MAKING CHANGE

A GUIDE TO EFFECTIVENESS IN GROUPS

Eileen Fay Nitzberg Guthrie
Warren Sam Miller

ISBN 0-917340-07-8

Designer: Robert Friederichsen
Editors: Jeanne Emrich and Ramona Starks
Illustrator: Barry Ives, San Francisco
Printer: Printing Arts, Inc.

INTERPERSONAL
COMMUNICATION PROGRAMS, INC.
300 Clifton Avenue
Minneapolis, Minnesota 55403
(612) 871-7388

This book is dedicated to
our primary colleagues and friends,
William Grimberg and Mike Groh

PREFACE:

During recent years, we have noticed a shortage of written materials relevant to people who are involved in citizen participation and self-help movements now going on in this country. MAKING CHANGE was written to provide a conceptual framework and practical ideas to approach community development and bring about positive change.

We use a "leadership development" approach, oriented toward teaching people the skills they need to gain power and manage change in their lives. We intentionally did not try to focus on specific issues (e.g., tenant rights, child care, tax reform); rather, we chose to focus on skills and concepts that could be adapted to any issue and any group situation. We call our body of ideas "process politics."

As co authors, there are a number of issues on which the two of us have different opinions. But, as we worked together on this book, we found we held a common commitment to democratic processes of change. In order to give some idea of our perspectives in regard to MAKING CHANGE, we'd like to share our "basic raps."

Eileen sees MAKING CHANGE as a tool for advocating and supporting the development of grassroots leadership. With appropriate assistance, people who now see themselves as victims of institutional and bureaucratic systems can develop the self-confidence essential for social change efforts to have long-range effectiveness.

Sam's reason for writing the book is his interest in empowerment at all levels, not just the grassroots. His experience has shown that, to a great extent, people in City Hall, the private sector, and the community all benefit from a sense of increasing the control they have in their own lives. The framework he uses to look at the process of empowerment is called "human energy ecology"—how people make use of their energy as individuals, in relationships, and in groups.

We each want to make special mention of the people who have taught us the most about what has come to be called process politics. Thanks, from Eileen, to: Barbara Anderson-Sannes, Bill Grimberg, Kebie Hatcher, Glenna Krause, Margaret Macneale, Orville Mestes, Sam Miller, Mike Roan, and Dennis Wynne. Thanks, from Sam, to: Betty Aldridge, Hartz Brown, Mike Groh, Bristow Hardin, Don Klein, daughters Brenda and Laurie, parents Levi and Nina Miller, Carl Smith, David Rogers, and Wheelock Whitney.

We hope the ideas offered in *MAKING CHANGE* are helpful to all people working to build strong communities. Also, as more and more people begin to understand the importance of how decisions get made, we hope that together we can all contribute to creating and implementing our collective visions of how our lives and our communities can be.

We welcome thoughts, comments, and criticisms about the material included in *MAKING CHANGE*.

Eileen Guthrie and Sam Miller
March 23, 1978
Minneapolis, Minnesota

CONTENTS

CHAPTER 1.

INTRODUCTION: PROCESS POLITICS — A NEW WAY TO THINK ABOUT COMMUNITY CHANGE

Process politics is a new approach that groups and communities can use to get things done in a way that builds in accomplishment and personal fulfillment. It includes operating definitions, based on how people and communities function. It includes theory and techniques, learned from practical experience, about how to bring about community change. And it includes an outlook that emphasizes the possibilities for managing change creatively.

Process politics is a lot like writing a book. It's exciting, complex, frustrating, and educational. The rewards for the process politician and for the community can be great.

Late in 1975, the two of us got together at Sam's house. We had been friends for three years, but this was the first time in a while that we'd seen each other. We spent a couple of hours talking— sharing what we'd been doing over the past few months and comparing notes about our work with communities and groups.

As we talked, we started teasing about how we really ought to write up some of our experiences. After all, we reasoned, we do know a lot about doing community development work and, surely, there would be other people who would benefit from what we had been learning. The teasing tone changed; and we soon found ourselves giving serious consideration to the idea of being authors.

Writing a book would give us a chance to look more closely at our experiences, to consolidate our learning both for ourselves and for the benefit of others. Besides, working on such a project would give us an excuse to spend time together regularly, and we both wanted that.

The idea of doing a book was exciting and frightening. Neither of us had done it before, and we had little idea how to do it. After much discussion, we decided that we wouldn't let our ignorance stop us. We would write a book, and we would learn how to do it as we went along.

We talked a lot, building up a collection of notes as we worked. Those notes were sorted out, literally by putting pieces of paper into piles that seemed to fit together. We talked some more and finally began writing it all up.

Disagreements arose once in a while. And we would stop what we were doing and try to resolve the issue before proceeding. Personal problems came up, too; and together we talked them over and tried to help each other out.

We signed several contracts with each other during the writing. One was a commitment to complete our outline and chapter summaries by June; another was a commitment to have our manuscript done by January 1977. We worked hard on those contracts, and we stuck to them.

Most of you probably deal with projects like this every day. Sometimes, they're personal projects like writing a book. Sometimes, they're community matters like getting better garbage collection. But the basic question is still the same: HOW DO WE GET FROM HERE (the present situation) TO THERE (the desired goal)?

That's what this book is about: Figuring out how to get from here to there, in a way that moves us toward our long-term goal and at the same time provides us personal satisfaction, fun, and learning.

GETTING THERE IS AS IMPORTANT AS BEING THERE

The book-writing story suggests a central theme of process politics: The way things happen is as important as what happens.

It is no longer appropriate to argue about whether "means" are more important than "ends"; in process politics, they have equal importance.

We call the "end" the GOAL and the "means" the PROCESS. Once we had agreed on the goal of writing a book, we could focus on the process of planning our writing: What steps would we have to go through to end up with a finished book? How would we learn to do those things? Would we be able to work well together? All these and more questions needed to be answered.

In this book, we want to share some things we have learned about the processes that are involved in doing things with people. We have several premises that we believe in about working with people:

- Everybody counts.
- Feelings are facts.
- Everybody's perceptions are true, for them.
- Self-interest is okay.
- Power is amoral, neither good nor bad.
- Diversity is valuable in decision making.
- People can solve their own problems.

HOW COMMUNITIES OPERATE

A community is a group of people who have something in common. It might be a group who share common living spaces—such as a neighborhood, a commune, or a monastery. It might be a group with similar values—such as a church denomination or an academic institution. It might be a group of people who all have the same problem, such as a welfare rights organization or Alcoholics Anonymous.

Take a few minutes to think about the primary communities you belong to. Figure out which of those you belong to by choice, which by accident; which you can change, which you can't; which other people know about, which they don't.

_____

_____

_____

_____

Now, use the examples which you listed for yourself as you consider the following list of characteristics that we use when we think about communities. You might disagree, and you might have additions. The list represents what we have learned but is not a closed list!

1. A community is composed of lots of different kinds of people and opinions.

Each member of a community has had a particular set of experiences which is unique. From that set of experiences, he or she has developed a personal value system and certain feelings. For example, Don and Elizabeth are both residents of the same neighborhood and live in the same apartment building. But when the downstairs tenant (who is Native American) got evicted, Elizabeth was happy about not having any more Indians in the building, and Don was angered and accused the landlord of discrimination.

2. People in a community seldom agree on what's "right" and what's "wrong."

Even though a community is a group of people with some things in common, they don't have everything in common. Arguments break out within families; and neighbors disagree on whether the schools should be involved with sex education. Yet, family members and neighbors are part of the same community.

3. Every community has some things in it that are going well.

Often, we concentrate our efforts on criticizing and trying to figure out what we can complain about. That's not enough. We have to consciously look at what is working, too, so that we can keep those as parts of our community. As an example, the board of directors of a community center has been bogged down in disagreements over whether or not to take on responsibility for a new department. It's important for that group to remember that, although they do not agree, they are able to talk with each other about their disagreements. That is a positive factor that needs to be continued.

4. Every community has some things in it that are going wrong.

It probably isn't too hard for you to focus in on some of the problems in your community. What's important is to recognize that no community is perfect and, in fact, all. communities have times when things aren't going well.

5. Members of a community can help change things that are going wrong, although in actuality only a few of those members will do the work.

We've all seen situations where there seems to be lots of concern about how to deal with an undesirable situation. When the time comes for volunteers, though, few people come forth. Everyone else has some reason for not becoming involved. It's our opinion that this is an inevitable situation. Not everyone has the interest, time, or optimism to work for change. Those who do have the inclination must be responsible representatives and not just act for themselves.

6. Communities are affected by outside forces over which they have little immediate control.

Sometimes, in today's world of technology, it seems that there is nothing we cannot control. But then a natural disaster, such as a tornado or a severe drought, hits the headlines. And we are reminded that, in fact, we do not have all the answers.

7. Each community fits into a larger context, as a particular individual fits into the family system of his or her birth.

Events that happen outside a community can directly affect that community and, conversely, events within a community can have an external effect. To put it simply, no community exists in a vacuum. We all share a common, interlocking interest to some extent.

8. Communities don't change overnight.

No matter how much we hope for a "fair" system, the possibility for sweeping change to occur is slim. There is just too much personal and communal history and experience for there to be broad change that is quick. Community members who try to accomplish too much, too fast generally burn themselves out and quickly become cynical and ineffective.

9. Communities grow, learn, and develop.

We believe that communities go through phases of development that, in many ways, parallel the stages of human development. A newly-formed committee, for instance, is dependent on its leader (parent) for guidance and nurturing. As the group develops, there is usually a period of rebellion against the leader (adolescence) followed by a period of cooperation (maturity). This developmental phenomenon is sometimes re-experienced as new members are brought in and old members drop out.

CHANGE: FRAMEWORK FOR ACTION

It is important that communities and community workers understand change. In doing workshops over the past several years with community and organization people, we discovered that a person's attitude about change is the key. We asked groups to list words that suggest and/or define change. The lists included words such as:

alter
mutation
variation
transformation
re-evaluation
revolution
alternative
displacement
convert
growth
modify
reverse

Then, we asked people to indicate their emotional response to each word—whether positive, negative, or neutral. What we found was that, even with people who identified themselves as "change agents", there were often more negative than positive connotations to the change words they listed.

When we asked them to indicate the attitudes of their communities for the same list of words, we found a much stronger negative response. We expected this since it is predictable that people trying to manage change would be more positively oriented towards it than the general population. What surprised us was that there was such a high degree of negative response by the change agents themselves.

We believe that change is inherently neither positive nor negative, but it may be either when viewed from the perspective of a particular situation. We agree with Alvin Toffler, author of *Future Shock,* that we live in a time of rapid and accelerating change, for individuals, relationships, communities, and cultures.

The key issue in understanding change is not to decide whether change itself is good or bad but to examine the effect that a specific change will have upon the needs, values, goals, and interests of a person, group, or community. This is sometimes a difficult task because the self-interests and goals of a community of diverse persons and groups may be in direct conflict with one another (see Chapter 9).

We believe that new approaches to managing change are needed at all levels of decision making. There are many examples of change being directed toward the benefit of small groups of people with vested interests in the outcomes. Too many people feel like losers in relation to the changes that affect their lives. Process politics provides a perspective that can open up the management of change to large numbers of people and provide a community with access to the problem-solving energies of its own members.

APPROACHES TO CHANGE

Now that we've given some introduction about how we view change—as inevitable, neither good nor bad, manageable—we'd like to examine some of the ways to apply those theories to our work in neighborhoods and communities. The notion of organizing our thinking about change so that we can manage it is not a new one; many people over the years have written and practiced different appraoches to bringing about desired changes.

In the case of the labor movement activities, the *confrontation approach to* creating change was often evident. Saul Alinsky, who developed a framework for planning social action using this model, is a person that is frequently associated with this style of managing change. The objective is for an organizer to help people who feel oppressed to form "people's organizations" to confront decision makers so that some desired change is made. The confrontation model is based on a we/they perspective, allying grassroots people against their common enemies.

A group of depositors with accounts in the same bank got together and decided that they wanted the bank to begin giving out more home mortgages to people in their neighborhood. They called a press conference, to which the bank directors were invited and demanded publicly that the bank disclose the zip codes for where outstanding mortgages were held. The depositors threatened a broad-based boycott of the bank if such disclosure was not provided.

Many groups use the *New England town meeting format,* where decisions are made by a legislative body that is open to all adult members of the community. Decisions are made by the rule of the majority. In large communities, individuals cast their votes through elected representatives. The representatives are accountable to their constituents, primarily at election time. This model has recently been running into criticism by minorities and women, who feel that their voices cannot be heard through a system that depends so thoroughly on majority vote.

Because of the problems connected with majority-rule legislative remedies, the *party politics* approach to organizing for change is very strong in all parts of the country. Party politics is basically a refinement of the legislative model mentioned above, where coalitions of community people and their representatives form around issues, personalities, and philosophy in order to achieve majority votes on key concerns.

Since the disturbances and riots of the 1960's in many of our inner-city neighborhoods, a number of civil rights leaders and community activists have become involved in the party politics of their precincts and districts. From that position, they feel better able to exert influence on their legislators.

The *community action approach,* popularized during the Great Society days of Lyndon Johnson, is another way to involve communities in managing change. Federal dollars were made available so that grassroots people could be hired to develop services and solve problems that were directly affecting their lives. The doctrine of "maximum feasible participation of the poor" that emerged from the so-called War on Poverty relies on funds and support from government while, at the same time, emphasizing self-help by residents.

Communities still are struggling with the concept of community action and what it means. To many it means jobs for their neighborhoods. To others, it includes outreach and delivery of advocacy and counseling services. To still others, it means local control of institutions in the community such as schools or police.

What happens when decisions are made that promote change in directions that conflict with community needs? Communities are becoming aware that *judicial remedies* can be very helpful, in the form of class action suits, court injunctions, and other uses of the court system. Judicial remedies are expensive and very time-consuming—factors which may be viewed as either advantageous or a hindrance, depending on the situation and which side you are on.

A city council passed a motion authorizing a nationally-known discount store to build an in-town facility that required the closing of a major city street. Citizen groups organized and hired a lawyer to begin proceedings to demand a full environmental study to determine how the proposal would affect residences and businesses in the surrounding area. All further construction on the site has been delayed until the court rules on the matter.

Dr. Martin Luther King, Jr. is a person associated with yet another approach to managing change: *civil disobedience*. Civil disobedience tactics call attention to perceived injustices through organized, non-violent action. An example is the Montgomery, Alabama bus boycott which successfully challenged the tradition that black patrons could only ride in public busses if they sat in the back.

The women's movement and evangelical Christianity are two examples of a *consciousness-raising approach* to achieving change. This model assumes that broad change occurs only after individual values are changed. Under this philosophy, organized efforts at social and political change are considered less important than personal enlightenment.

There are valuable elements in all of the above-listed ways to manage change. But we feel that, in and of itself, each approach is inadequate.

OTHER APPROACHES TO EFFECTING CHANGE

We went through lots of discussion about how to deal with such violent approaches to change as rioting, military coup, assassination, and revolution.

Yes, these tactics do exist, and they are used—under the philosophy that "the end justifies the means." We mention these approaches because they exist. But we question the long-range value and the ethics of such methods and personally do not advocate the use of violent strategies.

PROCESS POLITICS: THE ART OF THE POSSIBLE

"Process politics" is the name we have invented for our perspective on change and how to manage it. As a body of techniques, process politics draws on those change-management approaches outlined above. Process politics places importance on all of the following goals:

Goal 1. To influence institutional, as well as individual, causes of community problems.

The Welfare Rights Organization has gotten five phone calls within the past two days complaining about the way food stamps are being allocated by the local welfare office. One way of looking at the situation would be to demand that the present staff be fired; the "process politics" approach would be to examine, in addition, how much of the situation is caused by bad policy and needs to be addressed from that standpoint if the problem is to really be solved.

Goal 2. To encourage self-determination.

In process politics, we believe that groups and communities need to recognize and build on their own expertise and skills as much as possible. They need to decide for themselves what their futures will be like. We believe that people grow and learn best when they have the opportunity to determine their own successes—and failures.

Goal 3. To increase cooperation within and among communities.

The world is very small these days. And yet there are many times when we don't really know what's going on down the block, much less across town. Since many of the actions that *my* community group gets involved with could potentially affect *your* group, process politics encourages communications and regular contact among groups interested in the same problems. Without such opportunities for contact, we might never find out that we are operating on incorrect (or correct) assumptions about one another's intents and purposes.

Goal 4. To develop individual skills.

Too many times, community organizers come into our neighborhoods to "help us help ourselves." But just think: How many of those community organizers have really taught us skills that we needed to learn to do community organizing on our own? We believe that unless an organizer's role includes increasing residents' skills at problem-solving and figuring out how to get what they want, the organizing effort tends to be short-lived and discourages self-determination.

Goal 5. To spread ownership of decisions by involving large numbers of people in decision-making processes.

In process politics, a component of effective decisions is that the decisions "stick." That is, there are enough people who feel a strong commitment to a particular decision that they work hard to follow through. We have found that even "good" decisions do not get carried out unless they have committed backers. Process politics considers it essential that everybody's opinions get heard and built into the group's decisions.

Goal 6. To value individual differences.

We are continually amazed at the richness of decisions that are made by very diverse groups of people. In process politics, we place a high value on having many different kinds of folks involved in deciding things, and we use techniques to encourage that involvement.

THE FOUNDATION BLOCKS OF PROCESS POLITICS

As we worked on crystalizing some of our thoughts about process politics, we constantly found ourselves stopping to question what our basic assumptions were. We knew these assumptions would be the backbone of process politics as we defined it: *Process politics is a set of assumptions and techniques to help communities manage their own processes of growth and development toward becoming capable, effective problem-solvers.* But what assumptions, ideas, or notions were we operating with as foundation blocks?

To begin with, we believe that *problems are solvable.* Process politics can be thought of as the "art of the possible." Sure, not all problems are solvable right now; but we have a basically optimistic attitude about people's abilities to figure out a logical way to approach difficult decisions.

Second, we believe that both *creative energy and pragmatism are essential components in solving problems.* It's important for communities to know what they want, what can be done—now, and what can be done—later. Creativity is important in helping free people from tunnel-vision thinking, where they unconsciously limit their options. Pragmatic thinking helps keep the group in touch with realities that might make reaching goals easy or more difficult.

Third, we believe it is essential to pay attention to both *long-term perspectives and short-term objectives.* We have learned that communities need to define their long-range goals (e.g., getting a community center and staff into their neighborhood) but, unless they have short-term checkpoints along the way to gauge their progress, they may give up long before the final goal is accomplished. People need payoffs, frequently, if they are to continue working toward something.

Fourth, we recognize that *many different approaches to change are useful,* depending on the situation and its dynamics. We believe that some people respond to consciousness-raising approaches, while others are more effectively involved through an educational process. The acceptance of different approaches implies that we believe it is important for communities to decide which approach is most appropriate for a particular situation.

Fifth, we believe that *people count.* They are more than numbers in any group. They have personalities and experiences that affect how they respond and what they contribute. This assumption means that it is important to notice people, to relate to them as individuals with individual wants, hopes, and fears. It is also important to relate to people as members of groups, with group wants, hopes, and fears. Mr. James might very well be the director of the City Health Department, but he is also a human being who has good and bad days and who sometimes doesn't get home from meetings until 11:00 at night.

And, sixth, we believe that *it is important to learn from what we do.* Sam tells a story about when he was learning to ski. He decided that it was okay to fall down once because he looked the wrong way, but if he fell down *twice* because he looked the wrong way, that was stupid. That's why we try to talk a lot about what we are doing, and how, and why we make the choices we make. If something isn't going right, we sure don't want to go on until we've tried to figure out what's going on and how to make it better. Also, if something has gone well, it's important to take a look at what made it work.

A LOOK AT POWER

Power is a loaded word: Most people have emotionally-charged responses when they are in a situation with perceived power struggles. This is true in one-to-one relationships as well as in groups.

We have been doing training for several years using the "Power Lab", a group simulation of community dynamics in which people belong to different groups in a workshop (see Chapter 11). The groups have unequal access to things they need or want (like food, space, beds, etc.). One group has control over resources other groups want or need.

There are many interesting stories about things that happen in a power lab. Very few people feel comfortable with the power differences, but one thing is common to all groups: They respond. People experiment with various ways to get their group together and to influence other groups. Some become aggressive, others withdraw, others strategize. All the models for managing change are tried. Sometimes groups use their power to help solve problems; often, they have trouble knowing what to do with it.

The power lab has taught us several things about power:

There is nothing inherently bad (or good) about power. The key issue is: "How is power used?."

It is unlikely that a group is totally powerless in a situation. A helpful perspective is to change from, "Isn't it terrible how powerless I am?" to "How can I influence *this* situation?."

Feelings of powerlessness often come from untested assumptions. Information shared directly between groups "tests" assumptions and gives people real data to act on—clarifying issues and increasing possibilities for cooperation. Too much energy is wasted acting on assumptions about what the "other side" is doing.

We believe that a group's effectiveness in problem-solving can be enhanced by working with a grid perspective instead of an either/or one. "I'm right" does not always mean "you're wrong." If we assume that "I'm right" *and* "You're right," then an either/or perspective simply doesn't fit.

Either/or Perspective: I'm right ·· · · · · · · · · · You're right

If our framework is a continuum, as shown above, then resolution of our differences must take the direction of whoever is stronger, or craftier. To the extent that you win, I lose.

Our model looks like this:

Grid Perspective:

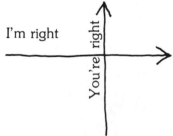

The "grid" framework allows us to work with the probability that we are both right. The resolution can be more collaborative and meet at least some of both our needs.

We learned about the grid approach when we were doing community development training at the University of Minnesota. Sam had been working with community organization and organization development, from a political systems approach, trying to effect change in institutional practices. His co-worker, Mike, had been working in counter-cultural agencies and focused on individual lifestyle and values. After several months of conflict, each accusing the other of not being very bright, they realized that it was possible to integrate both perspectives and generate alternatives for their work which were not available in an either/or framework. Their energy could then be directed towards answering questions like, "How is Sam right" or "How is Mike right?"

An important factor in working with power issues is to keep in mind the differences between formal and informal power structures. We use "formal power" to mean the influence people have because of their position (elected official, director, chairperson, etc.). "Informal power" is influence that is not defined by the organizational chart. "Informal power" is determined by things like age, talkativeness, wealth, friends, etc. and often has a greater impact on groups than the formal structure. It is also more difficult to identify.

One way to find out about a group's informal power structure is to ask three randomly-selected group members the question: "Who are the three most influential people in this group?" That will give you a possible list of nine names. Ask those nine people the same question. The possible 27 names will include. duplications. By counting the number of times each name appears, you have a rough idea of where the informal power lies.

A basic understanding of power, of how change happens, and of how communities function provides a sound beginning for effective community action efforts. And, since everyone is involved in a group of some kind, the group provides a good setting for us to use in talking about how change happens, how decisions get made, and how power gets used. Community change efforts require working with groups, and effectiveness in groups is linked very closely with effectiveness in relation to issues.

References for Chapter 1:

Saul Alinsky, *Rules for Radicals* (New York: Random House, 1971).

John Kenneth Galbraith, *Economic Development* (Cambridge, Mass.: Harvard University Press, 1964).

Michael Harrington, *The Other America* (New York: Macmillan, 1962).

Alvin Toffler, *Future Shock* (New York: National General Company, 1971).

PART 1

SELF-AWARENESS

One of the things that helps a group be effective in achieving its goals is for group members to make good use of their personal attributes. A conscious process of self-awareness by individuals and groups makes them both more effective. By paying attention to our own patterns, values, strengths, and relationships, we are able to appreciate the actions and feelings of others. This awareness can help group members work with each other instead of against each other and contribute to overall group effectiveness.

Chapter 2 describes a variety of leadership functions needed to help groups be effective. The process politician views leadership as a set of functions, or roles, that are shared by members of a group, not as a position that someone occupies.

Chapter 3 suggests several ways to look at personal needs and group involvements. Being clear about our own values, strengths, and motivations can help us choose group activities in which we will be effective.

Chapter 4 focuses on the importance of having an on-going support group. A regular support network can help prevent the tendency toward burn-out and loss of perspective that sometimes afflicts community workers.

CHAPTER 2.

WHO WE'RE TALKING ABOUT:
THE PROCESS POLITICIAN

Many people have commented about the work that we do as agents of change. They comment about the things we have helped to accomplish by giving support to their efforts for change.

People notice that we're involved in lots of different activities, that we have a broad range of interests, and that we are able to get things done. But we feel it's essential not to do everything ourselves. The secret of being effective as a process politician is to draw on the resources and abilities of all community residents, to come up with accurate diagnoses and action plans for various situations in our communities.

It's important to distinguish between being *effective* and being *efficient*. Much of our modern-day society puts a high premium on efficiency (fast, cost-effective, product-oriented thinking). We contend that being effective community change agents calls for a different approach, one that considers both process and goal. *How decisions get made is just as important as what the final decision is.*

It is the responsibility of process politicians to help their community to be conscious of process concerns: to solicit ideas from many different sources, to help people express and deal with their feelings about their involvement in community concerns, to encourage the community to explore alternatives before deciding on a course of action, and to assist folks in making use of self-interest issues as they work together to get what they want.

It is not necessary for anyone to have the title "process politician" to be able to act in that role. Sometimes, it is effective to
function unobtrusively, as a group member who calls the group's
attention to process as a way of achieving goals. People can share
the functions of a process politician. It doesn't matter whether the
function is performed by one person or by many; what does matter is that someone be concerned about how decisions are being
made and how the group is functioning.

We believe the best decisions take into account both long and
short-term effects and are decisions that many people have a part
in formulating. The process politician helps get ideas out into the
open, by helping people understand the value of hearing many
points of view. Two people can come up with a plan, but if two
more were consulted, that would mean two additional points of
view that could be built into carrying out the agreed course of action. The planning process takes longer for four people than for
just two, but we found that the extra time is worth it because you
get better decisions in the first place.

An important part of being an effective process politician is to
deal with emotional as well as political realities. The process politician helps group members to consider people's feelings and to
know that it is okay to do so within the context of a meeting
room. If one group member simply states that he or she is confused about what is going on and asks for help, it is easier for
others to share *their* feelings. One measure of effectiveness in
working with groups is to check out whether or not people need
time to "unwind" after meetings. A group whose members can go
home with a feeling of accomplishment and a clear sense of direction is more effective in that regard than a group whose members
need two hours to unwind before they can get to sleep.

This does *not* mean that every group member needs to share
the details of their most recent family spat. That's not a community concern and is irrelevant to the business-at-hand. But it does
mean that a process politician's responsibility includes helping
community members express feelings and reactions to issues
under discussion and to the dynamics of the meeting itself.

The process politician can also assist in compiling ideas and
concerns from different people so that the community can begin

to develop action plans. It is important to remember that a process politician is not primarily a decision-maker but, rather, is a provider of assistance to help people make decisions on their own. We believe that group members always know more about their own group, their problems, and their direction than any outsider possibly can. The process politician acknowledges that expertise is not a matter of academic degrees but is a matter of our life experiences as human beings.

Another part of being a process politician has to do with working with people so that they learn to be aware of their own motivations and the motivation of other individuals or organizations. Part of community action depends on building action strategies that accept various motives and interests.

Effective community action has to do with how well people's time and energies are utilized, how clearly people can express their expectations and work to fulfill them, and how flexible group decisions can be. A group can best succeed in reaching its goals when the expertise and humanness of its members is tapped. Process politicians have the job of supporting a community's growth and development so that individuals are listened to and decisions are made which reflect the thinking of a broad cross-section of that community.

ROLES OF THE PROCESS POLITICIAN

Change agents—people who use their energy to work for change— come in many different styles. A communist revolutionary who stands on the street corner and distributes leaflets is as much an agent for community change as a community organizer who teaches people to band together to achieve their mutual goals. Some change agents are *employed* to work for change (consultants, counselors, organization development specialists); and others are *volunteer* community members (legal aid lawyer, planning council member, block club leader).

Process politicians, paid or volunteer, are *change agents* by definition and help people in communities become more capable of solving their own problems effectively. They help people learn to be better leaders who can then increase a community's abilities to achieve its desired goals. The particular change which process politicians work to bring about is more openness in decision-making processes and, thus, better decisions. For process politicians, the outcomes and decisions themselves are secondary to the process by which those outcomes and decisions are reached.

Sam was asked to be a consultant to the board of directors of a halfway house. His contract stated that he was to help the group work together better, without taking sides or advocating a particular direction or position.

Eileen got elected to serve on a citizen advisory committee to advise the City Council on how to spend Community Development Block Grant funds. Since she was new to community development and housing issues, she decided to make use of her expertise in process techniques while she became more familiar with the substance of the discussions. She "volunteered" to deal with decision-making openness.

Process politicians sometimes function as *educators*, to help a group see itself more clearly or provide individual consultation to a community board member. These functions differ, depending on the situation.

Eileen was asked to teach decision-making skills and conflict resolution techniques to a group of community leaders. She presented them with a series of workshops, geared to help them look at their own styles of participating in problem-solving.

The educator does not have to be seen as a traditional teacher, who stands in the front of a group and lectures about theory. Rather, the process-politican-as-educator uses a variety of teaching techniques, including small-group discussions, films, experiential-learning exercises, and written materials. It is useful for a process politician to know some group decision-making and personal dynamics theory as a framework from which to operate, however. We find that theory is much more useful if the process politican has experiences with which to relate the theories.

The process-politician-as-educator demonstrates ways in which to obtain group consensus, advises a community organization president on how to run a successful meeting, and helps people learn about community resources and issues. Since the process politician may be in contact with many different people during any particular week, the opportunities for informal education and information sharing are also great.

When someone calls Sam for advice in preparing a grant proposal and how to get it funded, Sam is aware of that request as an opportunity to teach some process-oriented skills as well. He may bring up the issue of self-interest or open participation in decisions, as a way to increase awareness and do some community education.

Eileen, as chairperson of the planning council for her community, "models" styles of openness in discussing issues. She checks frequently during meetings to see if anyone is feeling cut off or misunderstood, and encourages group members to express disagreements so that all points of view are taken into account.

There are occasions when a process politician is called on to be an *advocate* for a community. This might include speaking to a city council sub-committee about the problems in the neighborhood, or helping a next-door neighbor get needed medical care. Advocacy could also include taking public positions in support of open decision-making processes.

Both Sam and Eileen are often heard extolling the virtues of "process" and citizen participation. This book is an example of the process-politician-as-advocate for a particular position. We are trying to sell our ideas to you.

Whenever we try to get funding for a project or proposal that we are interested in, we are acting as advocates for a certain point of view or a certain program. We don't take on projects that we can't advocate on a personal level.

The process-politican-as-advocate can function as either a group member, a consultant, or a staff person. The techniques used by either can range from writing a letter to a city planning commissioner or visiting the welfare office with a client/friend in need of help. The choice of techniques varies with the situation.

Groups sometimes have a hard time seeing themselves. When a group gets so focused on its goals that the needs of its members and its internal dynamics are ignored, the *fair witness* role of the process politician becomes important. The fair witness helps a group by providing a mirror through which members can get an objective look at themselves as they work. By stepping out of the task discussions, the fair witness can give full attention to such things as who is talking, who is not participating, body language, whether or not people are listening to each other, etc.

Group members can be free to become totally immersed in certain tasks, knowing that a fair witness is on the job to help the group function. A group can ask for fair witness observations several times during a meeting, at the close of the meeting, or as they occur. It is important that the fair witness try to express observations objectively, avoiding judgments about what has been seen.

"I'm not sure Howard understood what Louise said," is a more useful statement than, "Howard should listen better when Louise says something."

The fair witness role can be performed by any member of a group or by a staff person. One useful way of incorporating this role into a group's life is to pass it around, asking a person with less interest in the subject under discussion to be a fair witness. Over time, every member of a group can have an opportunity to be fair witness, and the group's level of awareness about process issues can be increased.

Sometimes, a group becomes so focused on solving problems that it does not see all the available options. This is especially true when there is conflict which springs from an "either/or" approach to a problem. When this happens, the process politician can provide a helpful function as *option offerer*. The option offerer helps a group consider a variety of alternative solutions to a tough problem. Sometimes, it is useful for the group to brainstorm different ideas without discussing or judging them. One problem we have encountered is that groups that use only parliamentary procedure in their meetings may not be considering some good alternatives: once a motion is on the floor, the group's attention is limited to

that idea. We find that it is helpful to try listing several options before getting into the narrowing-down process of deciding what shall be done.

We have discussed several roles of the process politician: educator, advocate, fair witness, option offerer. All of these roles can be done whether the process politician is a member of the group or an outside consultant. These roles can be learned by group members who want to function more effectively.

POWER

How do questions of power relate to the discussion of process politician? As suggested in Chapter 1, we believe that it is critical to grapple with "power" as a pre-requisite for effective community action. Power is amoral, neither good nor bad in itself. Power can be given up, and it can be taken away!

The function of the process politician in relation to power is to help increase people's awareness and effective use of power. Unless people acknowledge and use their own power, they are giving it away to someone else. Sometimes this is inevitable, sometimes it is a conscious choice. *The important thing is to pay attention to what power you have and what power others have.*

Power takes many forms: passive, assertive, formal, or informal. Personal power can take the shape of having money, having a dynamic personality, having permission to speak for a group, or knowing the right people. Group power could include having many members, being designated an "official" representative of a certain viewpoint, being successful, or having access to information sources.

> The board of directors of a community program had to make a decision of whether to remain autonomous or become a department of a major hospital to ensure funding. The motion to join the hospital was made and seconded, but no one seemed ready to vote. Finally, the chairperson asked for the opinion of one of the original board members, who had not yet said anything. He spoke in favor of the motion, and the

motion passed. It was the chairperson's assessment that there would have been no action without that person's input.

As stated in Chapter 1, "power" is a loaded word. To most people, it has negative connotations. We define power as being neither good nor bad. *Power is the ability of an individual or group to influence other individuals or groups.* This happens all the time, in positive, negative, and neutral ways. We may often have difficulty determining whether a person is using power in a way which will help or hurt us. Usually, the tendency is to be suspicious until we understand the situation.

A community organization elected a new board of directors, some of whom were new to the organization. They questioned everyone about community issues, to check out whether they were getting biased or objective information. They were hesitant to rely on any single source of information until they knew more about that person. The new officers continued their questioning and asked the resource people to help bring the new folks on board.

How can power be used positively? Power can be used to get money for a neighborhood rehabilitation program, to make civil service jobs more available to minority or poor people, and to bring people together to identify goals they have in common. Unless a person or group accepts that power can be positive, they are giving up some of their own abilities to exert influence on others.

It is especially important for the process politician to understand the dynamics of power to help people realize their own power.

One way to get a handle on personal power is to list occasions in which you exerted influence. After that, compare lists with a friend and get comments about how effective that influence was.

HOW TO MAKE THE MOST OF YOUR ENERGY

Process politicians are often under pressure. They help resolve conflicts and try to be "on top of things" most of the time. The truth of the matter is that we make mistakes, change our minds, and have days when everything seems to go wrong. We have developed some "rules to live by" to minimize personal hassles doing community work and make the best use of our energy.

By keeping the basic "rules" in mind, it is easier to get through periods of frustration.

Rule 1. Go with the flow.

The key to going with the flow is to remember that life is lived in the here-and-now, each day at a time. We can relive yesterday only as a memory and experience tomorrow only in anticipation.

Energy spent in worry about what has happened before or in anxiety about what might happen in the future is energy that could be focused on making the most of the present moment.

Rule 2. Trust your hunches.

We believe in "plain common sense." The important thing is to get in touch with your hunches and follow what they tell you.

This rule is useful in getting through strategy sessions or conflict situations. It can be useful to express a hunch: "I don't know where this notion is coming from yet, but I have a hunch that we're missing the point." The other people involved can then help sort out the logic and examine whether the hunch is on target or not.

It's important not to hold back your opinions because you are afraid that someone will think you're stupid. If you limit yourself to logical comments, you are using only half your brain-power. Intuitive thinking in brainstorm sessions can be very useful and may spark some creative thinking or discussion by the group.

Rule 3. Learn from what you do.

We believe it is important for process politicians to learn personally from their activities. The more a process politician keeps learning, the more energy he or she seems to have. For us, there is a definite correlation between how much we are learning from our involvements and how much energy we have to give.

We ask ourselves some questions when we suspect that we've stopped learning from our work: Am I listening carefully to what's going on around me? Am I talking too much? Am I bored? How can I learn more from my present involvements? Are my present involvements appropriate for me, or should I consider dropping some? Am I saying "no" enough? What things could turn me on again?

It *is* okay to change interests, to get bored, and to want to move on to new areas of concern. Many community workers lose their effectiveness after being in the same arena for more than a couple of years. Regularly examining how much you are learning and whether you are losing effectiveness is essential for any process politician.

One way to keep learning is to consider everything you do as a course of study. In a meeting, you can study the ways groups operate; while cooking a meal, you can study the use of spices, etc. This approach to learning means that you are constantly aware of the variety of ways an experience can be viewed, with evaluation going on all the time. We get bored when we know what we're doing, so we do *new* things that we don't know how to do yet in order to keep on learning.

Rule 4. Keep your life in balance.

Everyone needs time for family, work, socializing, and being alone. Each of us has found that, when we're feeling off kilter, it's usually that we're giving too little attention to one of these areas of life. People differ in the amount of time needed for these things; but everyone needs time for contact with other human beings, for feeling challenged and productive, for having fun, and for contacting our inner selves.

The "right" balance of family/work/socializing/alone-time varies from person to person. You can figure out which needs *you* tend to shelve and how much balance you consciously should plan for.

TROUBLE SPOTS

We have experienced some pitfalls in working with communities and community workers that we think deserve special attention. Doing community work is difficult enough if everything goes well, and we hope that, by sharing some of the problems we have encountered, we can help you prevent some hassles.

One problem, not unique to process politicians, is a feeling of *helplessness* or impotence. This important area is developed more thoroughly in Chapter 10, "What to Do When You Don't Know What To Do."

Timing is another problem of group and community dynamics. We have seen ideas of good intention frustrated simply because the timing was bad.

A community planning group had recently added several new members and elected new officers. Several

veteran members were anxious to start the new year with some bold new activities and pushed for action. The new members, who still felt uncomfortable in the group, resisted the "pushiness" of the veterans. The veterans' ideas got soundly defeated until almost a year later, at which time they got unanimous approval.

Some people seem to have developed, by experience or intuition, a better sense of timing than other people. Our rule of thumb is that an idea whose time has come is one that relates to a need felt by several people in a group. We often "try out" an idea with a number of different people, to see if the timing is appropriate, before introducing it into a group. Otherwise, "trusting your hunches" is useful in judging when the time is right.

Trust is an important issue also. A process politician whose self-interests are not clear will have a difficult time helping open group communication. It is important to be clear, both with yourself and with other people, about what your personal interests are. If people feel in the dark about what you're really up to they will have trouble accepting your role as process politician.

For a group member or an outside consultant, a useful technique to initiate discussion when a group seems to be struggling with feelings of distrust is simply to say out loud that there appear to be suspicions and distrust within the group. Raising the issue publicly, at a group meeting, can be the first step in alleviating these concerns.

We have found that trust issues, like hidden agendas or suspicions, are best dealt with during the course of a group's activities, rather than by holding a special workshop or seminar on "trust."

While we believe that working with communities and groups is serious business, it is important to not take yourself too seriously. The ability to laugh at yourself is the key to avoiding this problem. When we make a mistake, or feel stuck, we find that it is better to stop, invite the group to join us in acknowledging our humanness, and go on by asking the group for help.

Sam uses an eleventh commandment to help him keep perspective at times like this: "Don't sweat the petty stuff." Recalling the commandment is very helpful in loosening people up.

Another area of concern is *confidential information*. Because process politicians talk frequently about the need for open communications, people tend to tell us personal concerns they have about a group or person. To avoid the temptation of using such information to manipulate situations, we encourage people to talk directly with each other, rather than use us as intermediaries. We may offer to help bring about a direct sharing of concerns between the two parties involved, but we refuse to get caught in the middle.

It is easy to get into trouble when we act on *assumptions* without checking them out. In planning for action, we treat assumptions as a starting point and often suggest that a group begin its planning by ascertaining what assumptions they are operating with and whether they are valid or not.

> Eileen's refrain for dealing with assumptions is, "Check it out."

A process politician can be involved in a variety of activities and have several roles. Specific roles and activities depend on the situation as well as your personal concerns as a process politician. It is important to be clear about who you are, what you want, and why you are doing what you are doing.

References for Chapter 2:

Chris Argyris, *Integrating the Individual and the Organization* (New York: John Wiley & Sons, Inc., 1964).

Eddy, et. al., *Behavioral Science and the Manager's Role* (Washington, D.C.: National Training Lab, 1969).

Robert Heinlein, *Stranger in a Strange Land* (New York: G. P. Putnam's Sons, 1961).

Watzlawick and Jackson, *Change* (New York: W. W. Norton & Company, 1974).

CHAPTER 3.

FIRST THINGS FIRST: KNOW WHERE YOU STAND

As we pointed out in Chapter 2, the process politician operates out of a number of different roles, from teacher to observer to advocate. We are called upon to switch roles numerous times during any particular day, depending on phone calls, which meetings are scheduled, or what the morning paper says. In addition to external factors, we have our personal needs and private lives to which we must pay attention.

How can a process politican cope with the potentially confusing situation of wearing such a variety of hats? Where can a process politician find stability in the midst of so many roles? Is there any universal answer to these questions?

The answer we have found is *self-acceptance*. We accept ourselves as human beings, with the capacity for achieving great successes—and great failures. We have emotions, needs, and limits. We change, learn, and interact with the environment constantly; and we need to have a stable base from which to operate.

Since it's hard to find stability in the world outside ourselves, it's important to look inward. If we know and accept who *we* are, it's a lot easier to know and accept other people for what *they* are. It's the same principle that Socrates taught his students thousands of years ago: Know thyself. Once I know who I am—at as many different levels as possible—then I have a basis for deciding if I want to change and, if so, in what direction.

Once you know yourself, then it's important to look at who you are in relation to others. Are your beliefs and goals consistent within themselves? Are they consistent with what other people in your community are saying? What can be done about any inconsistencies, if anything?

The 20th-century French novelist, Robbe-Grillet, wrote a story in which he describes a field. He stands inside the house and looks out of the jalousy window, and he presents one description. Then, he moves outdoors and looks at the banana trees in the field from another physical perspective. He keeps moving around and describing what he sees. Each description is different.

The above example illustrates an important reality: If we stand in only one position, we get only one point of view.

Part of the way to get a sense of perspective about ourselves is to listen to our "internal dialogue."

Someone called Eileen last week to invite her to a movie. She decided to go, but not before silently going through a series of considerations about whether she had time, if she wanted to see that particular show, or whether she wanted to do something else that evening. Each question—and each answer—revealed something about her personality and her needs.

Internal dialogue includes both emotional and rational parts. In working toward self-knowledge and self-acceptance, it is important to listen to both one's rational mind *and* one's "hunches."

An important ingredient of self-awareness is to experience the timeless qualities of the universe by "stopping the internal dialogue." There are many ways to do this: watching the sun set, traveling, meditating, worshipping, or even listening to music. In addition to renewing our energy, these experiences give perspective to everyday problems and help give us some distance from them.

Stop, close your eyes, and listen to yourself. How fast is your heart beating? Are you feeling warm or cool? What thoughts are going through your mind? Are your stomach muscles tense or relaxed? How does your body change with the changing mental pictures?

Everybody has ways of stopping the internal dialogue. Try listing some of the ways you have discovered. Then ask a friend how he or she does it.

SELF-AWARENESS AS A WAY OF LIFE

To process politicians, self-awareness is a way of life. It is a key to understanding ourselves and a bridge to understanding others.

The many approaches to self-awareness have been given different labels over the centuries. The philosophy of yoga, for example, teaches about the need to be detached from ourselves so that we can see our lives more clearly. Gestalt psychology helps individuals act out their internal dialogues so that they become more visible. Mind-expanding drugs sometimes heighten our awareness of ourselves and the universe around us.

One way to increase your self-awareness is to examine the five key dimensions of your experience: your senses, interpretations, feelings, intentions, and actions. These are always a part of you, but they are not always within your awareness. Increasing that awareness becomes a way of knowing yourself better and becoming more conscious of who you are. And it can increase your choice about yourself — to enjoy yourself as you are or to alter yourself — and increase your choice about whether or not to tell other people about yourself.

Your *senses* include your sight, hearing, touch, taste, and smell. They provide you with raw data that tells you what's happening around you. And they help you document your interpretations: "John's still tapping the table with his pencil. (Sense data) He must be nervous about the speech he's going to give. (Interpretation)".

Your *interpretations* are your thoughts, ideas, impressions, beliefs, opinions, evaluations and assumptions. In short, they are all the different kinds of meanings you make in your head to help you understand yourself, other people, and situations. The interpretations you make depend on the information your senses provide you and the thoughts you already have, as well as the immediate feelings, wants, and desires you bring into a situation.

Your *feelings* are emotional responses inside your body, though they may have outward signs. For example, when you feel angry inside, your outward signs may be tense muscles, flushed skin, loud and rapid speech, etc. Feelings are important in any situation and serve several functions. They can alert you to what is going on and help you understand your reactions to a situation. They also can help you clarify your expectations in a situation. (Some of your feelings are felt because of a difference between what you expect and what you actually experience). But feelings can only serve these functions if you let yourself be aware of them.

Your *intentions* can be anything from your immediate desire in a situation, to what you would like to accomplish during the day, to long-range goals for several years or a life time. Generally, it is the shorter term intentions that people have difficulty being aware of and disclosing to others.

Your *actions* are your behaviors — the way you speak, listen, move. Often you may not be aware of your actions. For example, your bodily posture, facial expressions, and voice characteristics are actions others may have observed in you but of which you have little awareness. It's hard to be aware of all your actions because so much is happening at one time. But your actions become sense data from which others make interpretations concerning you.

Of course, no one has total awareness of all these dimensions — not even for part of the time. Self-awareness is really a continuous process of discovery. One way you can help yourself in this process is to use a model called the Awareness Wheel. Many people have found it a very useful tool to help them think about what is inside themselves.

The Awareness Wheel[1] represents the five dimensions of your experience we've just discussed: your senses, interpretations, feelings, intentions, and actions. Its simple design is meant to be easy to visualize in your mind's eye as a reminder of all five of the dimensions.

---

[1]Sherod Miller, Elam W. Nunnally, and Daniel B. Wackman, *Alive and Aware: How to Improve Your Relationships Through Better Communication*, (Minneapolis: Interpersonal Communication Programs, Inc., 1975).

One way you can use the Awareness Wheel is to work your way around it, step-by-step as you consider a situation:

"I see a number of people gathering in the back of the room (sensing), and I think they might be working on an amendment to propose to the chair (interpreting). I feel very concerned about what it might be (feeling), and I want to help out if I can (intending). So I join the group (acting)."

You can start with any dimension first and examine as many or as few as you wish. The more dimensions you explore, the more complete will be your awareness.

Tune into your Awareness Wheel right now. Use it to examine a subject that has been on your mind lately. What are your feelings? Your intentions? Your thoughts? Your senses? Your actions? Asking yourself these questions will increase your awareness of this or any other subject and how it pertains to you.

The process of self-awareness is never-ending. We all change constantly, according to the situation in which we find ourselves at any given moment. Life is a constant state of flux, but we can adjust to its changing realities by being aware of what is going on within us at each moment.

How does self-awareness help us to be better process politicians?

Eileen knows that she needs approval from people around her. She has developed a style of leadership that builds on that need, rather than denies it. She encourages people to contribute their ideas early so that decisions she makes are more likely to reflect the community's viewpoints.

It is not important whether it is good or bad to need approval from others; what we are talking about here is recognizing who we are, whether we like it or not. In personal matters, as in communities, it is important to know what the situation *is* in order to move toward the situation as we want it to be.

People who work in community action efforts may say that talking about personal feelings is not appropriate in that context. We believe that self-awareness is the key to being an effective process politician and, thus, we say that dealing with feelings is not only appropriate but necessary. If members of a group feel confused, but no one says anything about it, the confusion continues. If, on the other hand, one person expresses the confusion and asks for help, then the group can provide more information towards resolution. It is important to keep in mind that people usually like to be asked for advice.

Eileen was working as a consultant to the chairperson of a community board of directors, prior to discussion of a critical issue. The chairperson was feeling worried about what might happen at the meeting. Eileen encouraged her to let the group know about her anxiety, as a way of taking responsibility for her feelings and as a way of letting others know that they, too, could express their feelings. The discussion went smoothly, and the group reached unanimity about the issue being considered.

Three individuals came to Sam recently and complained about their personal frustration with a community organization. They all felt left out by the leader's tendency to cut off discussion. Sam urged each of them to talk privately with the leader and ask him for help in dealing with their concerns. They suggested that he allow more time for discussing issues. He welcomed their comments.

PERSONAL POWER

Identifying your "personal power" is an important part of the self-awareness process since process politicians are so intimately involved with power issues. Taking time to look at your responses to power, your needs to exert influence, and your interest in building a power base is important in gaining an understanding of group struggles with those same concerns.

Wanting to exert power and influence is what community action and being a change agent is all about: When we are unhappy with the way things are, we want to exert our power and make things better. Remember, we have defined power as *the ability of an individual or group to influence other individuals or groups.*

A co-worker in community politics asked us the question, "How come, even though I know a lot of people who have power, I don't feel powerful?" Part of the answer has to do with self-awareness and recognition of the many ways she *has* exerted influence on others.

Another part deals with how successful or unsuccessful *others* see her efforts to influence the decision-making processes. It may be that she has unrealistic goals, and that she has trouble feeling influential unless she has accomplished all of them. Or it could be that she, in fact, doesn't use her skills effectively and that people do not listen to her at all.

Making the most of personal power can be viewed as figuring out ways to make the best use of yourself. What are your strengths? What are your weaknesses? How can you use your strengths more effectively in working for what you believe in? How can you minimize your weak points or, better yet, turn them into strengths? How can you use your power so that it benefits more people than yourself?

Your personal power base starts with you. If you know who you are, what your weak and strong points are, and where you are headed, then you will be more effective in getting what you want and helping others get what they want. The more you help others effectively get what they want, the more your personal power is increased.

THE INDIVIDUAL

We have talked in this chapter about the importance of knowing who you are. Now, we want to explore some ways of doing that. It's not easy to pursue a self-awareness program, but there are some tools that can be useful in getting started. It's best if you can try these exercises in a small group, or with a friend; but don't hesitate to do them on your own. You might then want to share your experience with someone else later.

Make a list of 10 phrases that describe who you are.

1. _____   6. _____

2. _____   7. _____

3. _____   8. _____

4. _____   9. _____

5. _____   10. _____

Now, go back over that list and decide which of the phrases describe (a) what roles you are in, (b) in-born characteristics, (c) personality qualities, (d) skills that you have, (e) other features about yourself.

People think of themselves in roles, as teacher, or parent, or secretary. But people also possess knowledge, feelings, a physical body, a set of values, and a spiritual reality that shape who we are.

Here's another exercise, to help look at how other people see you.

Make a list of 10 phrases that other people might use to describe who you are.

1. _____   6. _____

2. _____   7. _____

3. _____   8. _____

4. _____   9. _____

5. _____ 10. _____

How are your two lists the same? How are they different? If you are working with a group or friend, share your answers and ask for reactions about how they see you. Think about what you are learning about yourself from these exercises.

Another way to look at who you are, as a unique individual, is to consider you life experiences and what you have learned from them about yourself. The experiences in a life usually group themselves into what we call "natural chapters." For example, we experience childhood, adolescence, being a student, being married, changing jobs, etc.

Think about the chapters in your life and list the 5 major ones here.

_____

_____

_____

_____

_____

How did one chapter lead into the next? Were there sharp breaks between each chapter, or was there a flow from one to another? How long did each of the chapters last? What were the significant things that you learned while you were in each of the chapters? Can you predict what might be your next chapter? Talk with your friends about their chapters; chances are that each person's list will be quite different. This exercise can help you identify some of your *developmental* phases, still another way of looking at who you are.

Another part of you that is important to consider is skills. What can you do well? What do other people think you can do well? Ask some of your friends or family what they think of as your particular skill areas. Soak it in; too often, we overlook our skills! Also, think about what you want to learn to do better. Begin to improve your weak areas and turn them into strengths.

Focusing on personality traits is also a way of finding our more about who you are. List, either in writing or in conversation with a friend, the qualities that you possess—positive, negative, or neutral. Then, go through the list with the following questions in mind:

1. Which qualities are less used than others?
   Which are not readily available to you?
   Which are not shared much?

2. How do you stop yourself from using those qualities?

3. What could be good about sharing those qualities more?

4. Which qualities are you in charge of?
   Which are in charge of you?

Paying attention to questions like these increases self-awareness which, in turn, increases your personal power. That's where being an effective proces politician starts.

Knowing who you are is a first step. It is also important to take a look at *why* you do the things you do. Each of us has developed a value system for determining what we think is important in life. These values are our framework for deciding what we think is right or wrong, how to spend time, what to work towards.

Two people were comparing opinions on how best to prepare for the future. One person was convinced that the most important factor in planning ahead was financial security. That person was investing in real estate and insurance policies. The other person was convinced that the most important thing to consider was physical health. That person jogged five miles every day, swam regularly, and ate natural foods.

Neither of the people mentioned above has the complete answer.

Both have developed value systems which reflect how they decide what is important to them. Neither one is totally "right" or totally "wrong"; their value systems developed in response to their life experiences.

The theory of *values clarification* offers specific tools which help identify our own values and how they change over time. This last point is critical, as a reminder that we as human beings are in a constant state of growth and flux, necessitating continuous self-analysis of changing values and priorities.

The following exercise deals with clarifying your values on money, friends, alone-time, issues, and priorities.[1]

Make a list of 20 things you like to do. Then answer the following questions about that list.

1. If you had to stop doing 10 of the things, which would they be?
2. Which of the 10 things you would continue doing would be done alone? Which would involve others?
3. Which would cost more than $300 to do?
4. How often do you do your favorite things?

Personal integrity is important in process politics. We hear about government officials in conflict-of-interest disputes, about community activists who are discredited, about consultants who advocate their own beliefs. For the process politician, personal integrity is a key issue.

---

[1]Sidney B. Simon, Leland W. Howe, and Howard Kirschenbaum, *Values Clarification: A Handbook of Practical Strategies for Teachers and Students* (New York: Hart Publishing Company, 1972).

"Integrity," "personal ethics," "morality" are words that we don't hear much these days. Often, concepts of personal responsibility get down-played in favor of such ideals as "efficiency" or "progress" or "cost-effectiveness." It is our contention that effective process politics hinges on personal and professional integrity, even though the system in which we find ourselves can be amoral.

Are "pure motives" possible? Even if the answer is yes, we're not sure that's important. Integrity is simply a matter of being honest with yourself and straightforward with others.

> Eileen was asked how to achieve effective citizen participation. She advocated an independent "Office of Neighborhood Participation," to be set up as an advisory body to the City Council.
>
> Recently, she argued *against* that position because she learned additional information that changed her mind. To maintain her integrity, she explains how she happened to change her viewpoint in response to questions about this apparent change of position.

Sometimes, it is difficult to determine when to compromise, when to "sell-out," and when to push hard. Maintaining personal integrity is not always easy; but it can be made easier by dealing honestly with doubts and uncertainties as they occur.

We view the world as healthy and friendly. When we are uncertain about which course of action to follow, we ask ourselves which course is consistent with our original premise. If the proposal satisfies that initial review, then usually the question of personal integrity has been dealt with for now in such a way that feelings and opinions remain consistent and honest. This is a place where trusting your hunches helps.

What makes one person get involved in a particular issue, while others respond with apathy or indifference? The answer has to do with *self-interest — the most important concept in process politics.* Try the following exercise to help you get a handle on this concept.

> Think about a group you belong to. Ask a variety of people in that group why they are involved and what they are getting out of that involvement. Think about

why you are involved, and what your rewards are. Encourage people to be totally candid in their responses, to help you get a better understanding of motivation.

People often have a hard time answering questions about personal motivation. We have all been programmed to differentiate between "selfish" and "generous" activities, with certain connotations placed on these labels. "Selfish" actions are considered bad; and "generosity" is praised as a virtue.

We do not accept those definitions and value judgments. Understanding *and accepting* self-interest is the best way to deal with issues such as motivation, participation, and effective community action.

We define self-interest as the factors which act as rewards to an individual or group. Self-interest determines whether someone stays involved or leaves a particular situation.

People are motivated to do things either to earn money or to gain some other kind of personal satisfaction. Sam uses the word "monergy" to express incentives, sometimes because he gets paid cash and sometimes because of gains in energy or in learning. Any combination of money and energy that "feels" fair is adequate payment.

What am I being "paid"? That's often a good way to look at motivation. The answers might include: knowledge, meeting new friends, social activity, or a feeling of accomplishment; the answers might also include frustration, anxiety, or burn-out.

List activities that you are involved in within the community. Next to each one, state what you are getting out of that activity. Be honest!

Activity   *Pay-off*

_____

_____

_____

_____

Now, ask someone you know to do the same thing. Compare lists and talk about your pay-offs. You now have identified some of your own self-interest factors.

As a process politician, part of your responsiblity is to get people involved and keep them around. Understanding self-interest is the first step toward understanding people's motivation and reward systems. The succeeding steps of involving others will be dealt with later.

The notion of self-interest ties in with power and influence. A process politician who understands that everyone operates primarily out of self-interest concerns can make use of that principle in dealing with "power people" and community volunteers.

Dedication and pure altruism also play a role in process politics. We believe that anyone who claims to be acting out of unselfish interests is fooling him/herself and is likely to become fed-up, frustrated, and ineffective. This is not to deny the importance of high principles but, rather, points out that personal martyrdom wastes energy and promotes disillusionment and negativism.

Sam uses the phrase "syndrome of the cynical social worker" to describe professionals whose commitment to high ideals disguises their need for success, learning, and other self-interest payments. They develop cynical attitudes from denying these needs.

It is extremely important to reap personal benefits from involvement in community action activities. Without such rewards, it is ridiculous to expect anyone to stay involved for long.

An important dimension is to let other people know what your self-interest needs are. Saying honestly, "What I want to get out of this is _____," is helpful to everyone involved and makes the desired outcome more likely to happen. This lays out your agenda clearly and encourages others to do the same.

Everyone has so-called "selfish interests" for wanting to affect certain issues; but that is not, in and of itself, bad. In fact, unless we acknowledge what our own self-interests are, we're being unfair, dishonest, and—in the long run—ineffective.

WHO ARE YOU: THE CONTEXT

During the preceding pages, we talked about self-awareness and how others see you. In many ways, I *am* my relationships with others, and my interactions with other people and events shape who I am.

Also, in many ways I am what others perceive me to be, as in the old Scottish poem about wanting to see ourselves as others see us.

None of us exists in a vacuum.

> Picture a car engine with the carburetor removed. That carburetor may be perfect, but it is nonfunctional as long as it is detached from the rest of the engine; and the rest of the engine cannot work either. The engine comprises the "context", and it helps define what the carburetor is.

One way to get a picture of *your* context is to make a list of ten people you have learned from. These people are now a part of you; they helped define who you are. The challenge of figuring out how to make our community "engines" work well starts with taking a look at how we as individuals work in relation to our personal contexts.

A key to our personal context is *feedback*. The term "feedback" has a particular meaning with regard to process politics and self-awareness. Feedback is a way of helping another person to consider changing his or her behavior. It is communication to a person (or a group) which gives that person information about his or her effects on others. As in a guided missile system, feedback helps an individual keep behavior "on target" and thus better achieve goals.

Some criteria for useful feedback include:

1. It is *descriptive* rather than evaluative. By describing one's own reactions, others are left free to accept the feedback or not, as they see fit. By avoiding evaluative language, the potential for defensive reactions from others is reduced.

2. It is *specific* rather than general. To be told that you are "dominating" would not be as useful as to be told that, "Just

now, you did not seem to be listening to what others said, and I felt forced to accept your arguments or face attack from you."

3. It takes into account the *needs of both* the receiver and giver of feedback. Feedback can be destructive when it serves only your own needs and fails to consider the needs of the person on the receiving end.

4. It is *directed toward behavior* which the receiver has control over. People's frustrations are increased when they are confronted with short-comings over which they have no control.

5. It is *best solicited*, not imposed. Feedback is most useful when the receiver requests that input.

Feedback is a way of giving help. It is a corrective mechanism for individuals who want to learn how their behavior compares to their intentions. It is a means for establishing one's identity—and attempting to answer, "Who am I?".

The basic principle about giving and receiving feedback is that every one who interacts with us has some truth for us to hear, whether it is reinforcing or critical. Unless we are willing to listen to what others tell us about our behavior, we can't learn much about ourselves.

It is important to solicit feedback from others about yourself. A process politican who asks community members to freely offer criticisms and positive feedback sets an example at the same time as he or she requests personal learning opportunities.

Feedback can be solicited both formally and informally. Formal feedback occurs sometimes in the context of personnel evaluations. Informal feedback can occur when we pass others on the street or when we ask our closest friends to tell us how we came across at a panel presentation the other night.

> Eileen often sets up situations where she can receive feedback about her effectiveness. Before a speech, for instance, she asks friends to pay special attention to her style or manner of presentation so that they can suggest ways for her to improve the next time.

Sam likes to incorporate feedback into regular meetings. Often, at the end of a meeting which he has facilitated, he asks the group for responses about the meeting:

"I learned _____."

"I liked _____."

"I disliked _____."

Individual responses are written down on the board but not debated.

By giving *and* receiving feedback, we can learn about ourselves and our relationships with others. Giving feedback is an important part of helping each other to learn and grow. Groups, too, can learn about their behavior through a "process observer" who watches the group at work and offers feedback to the members.

In relating to our personal context, there are two basic positions. The *reactive* position finds us responding to issues that are presented to us for our reaction.

Mary does not know what is expected of her in her work as staff to a community group. The group accuses her of not being interested and not doing her job. Mary must *react* to these accusations.

The other position is what we call a *pro-active* one, where we initiate issues and take the offensive.

Mary realizes that she is under-utilized in her work with the community group. She is not sure what else she could be doing for them and decides to request a meeting with the steering committee to discuss her job, their expectations, and ways to work better together. Mary is in a *pro-active* position in this case.

The pro-active position described above is more likely to result in positive action, rather than polarizing the relationship between Mary and the group, complete with built-up resentments and accusations. We support being pro-active within the contexts in which we live and work, as a way to work towards meeting our own self-interests. The pro-active approach often results in shared problem-solving and avoids unproductive blaming.

With the concepts of self-interest, self-awareness, and pro-action we are now ready to discuss how to survive the community rat-race—without burning up all our energy or turning sour in the process of community development.

References for Chapter 3:

Carlos Castaneda, *Journey to Ixtlan* (New York: Simon & Schuster, 1972).

Haimowitz and Haimowitz, *Human Development* (New York: Thomas H. Crowell Co., 1960).

Alain Robbe-Grillet, *La Jalousie* (Paris: Editions de Minuit, 1957).

Sherod Miller, Elam W. Nunnally, and Daniel B. Wackman, *Alive and Aware: How to Improve Your Relationships Through Better Communication* (Minneapolis, Minnesota: Interpersonal Communication Programs, Inc. 1975).

Daniel B. Wackman, Sherod Miller, and Elam W. Nunnally, *Student Workbook: Increasing Awareness and Communication Skills* (Minneapolis, Minnesota: Interpersonal Communication Programs, Inc., 1976).

Louis Raths, Merrill Harmin, and Sidney Simon, *Values and Teaching* (Columbus, Ohio: Charles E. Merrill Publishing Company, 1966).

CHAPTER 4.

TAKING CARE OF YOURSELF: YOUR SUPPORT GROUP

Process politics is exhausting work. We see many community change agents burn out, to the point where they risk their mental or physical health if they don't drop out entirely. It is impossible to keep going forever at breakneck speeds. The question is how to be effective change agents who use energy wisely and avoid being ineffective or even counter-productive. The answer that we ask you to consider is in the *relationships* you'll find in a support group.

We have close friends who act as consultants to us in our roles as process politicians, and without them our lives would be harder and not nearly so rewarding. These people act as sounding boards, and they let us know when they see us getting in trouble or being inconsistent. They help us listen to the "truth of our critics", and they provide needed shoulders to cry on.

Support group members may be family members, next-door neighbors, or friends from school or work. They are the people we can count on to be there when we need them. Support group members share some of our interests and values. They are people who can understand why we get upset or excited without needing a detailed explanation of our reaction.

We have chosen heterogeneous support groups, with people from a variety of concerns and experiences.

Eileen's primary support group includes Sam (her co-author and mentor), Joan (a full-time student and wonderful listener), Charlie (a minister who works and lives in her neighborhood), Mary Kay (long-time friend who now lives on a farm in Wisconsin), Bill (co-worker and chef), and various others from time to time.

Sam's support group includes Mike (consulting partner), Laurie and Brenda (his daughters), Jeff (former roommate working in educational frontiers), Betty (close friend and student of psychic realities), Eileen (co-author and community activist), Rudy (yoga teacher and friend), and other friends, colleagues, former students, and mentors.

Be explicit in asking people to be part of your "support group." People are often flattered by such a request to be involved with

you and are eager to arrange the specific terms. The group members themselves may never meet and need not even be acquainted with one another.

It may seem contrived to actually ask people to be your personal supporters since it seems natural that our primary support comes from our family and friends. It is helpful to know that there has been an explicit agreement about what the relationship can include. In this way, you can build mutually helpful relationships that enhance your personal life as well as your effectiveness as a community change agent.

> Late-night phone calls are one of the okay activities between Eileen and people in her support group. Sometimes, she calls to seek advice or solace; other times, she just needs to get something off her chest.

Support group members can help us separate personal from community-related concerns. As process politicians, it's important to be aware of how our emotions affect our community work. This is hard to deal with honestly since it's difficult to be objective about our own behavior. At such times, calling on a support person can help us see more clearly what is going on with us.

> Eileen and a co-worker were hired as consultants to the community group in Eileen's neighborhood. She realized soon that her personal investment in the neighborhood was interfering with her ability to be an objective consultant to the group. She asked her co-worker to help her sort out her personal from her professional feelings as they continued work on the consulting contract.

A support group can help plan action strategies.

> Sam asks his support group to be sounding boards for his ideas about community issues. He doesn't wait until the ideas have hardened but, rather, calls on his supporters when ideas are in the early stages of development. In that way, he is more open to hearing criticism or suggestions. Sometimes, he gets new information that adds another dimension or changes his approach completely.

Eileen occasionally asks a member of her support group to preview a speech, review a letter, or suggest ways to deal with a power struggle. The objectivity that a "third party" can bring into a situation can be the difference between success and frustration.

BUILDING A SUPPORT GROUP

Everybody has a circle of friends who provide support of one type or another. Our purpose here is to take a look at who your informal support group is now, and to suggest some ways to expand that group to make it work better. If it is working for you, it is probably working for your friends also.

List the people you go to when:

1. You have a problem.

2. You want companionship and nurturing.

3. You want to play.

4. You want good feedback.

Now, look over the list of names you just wrote down. How many times are names repeated? Is there any overlap at all? Think about why this might be the case. Do you prefer to maintain distinctions between your private and your working lives? What other patterns or surprises do you notice when you look at the list of people you go to when you need someone?

We believe that relationships are tied to self-interest concerns and that we choose to associate with certain people because we anticipate certain rewards from those contacts. Our intent here is to point out the practical nature of personal relationships, not to de-mystify the beauty of good friendships and personal relations.

Interpersonal relationships are based on interpersonal pay-offs. The most satisfying and rewarding relationships are those in which we have a mutual give-and-take. Once we acknowledge that we are teachers *and* learners in our friendships, we can grow personally and enable others to grow as well.

Make a list of the people you learn from and what you learn from each of them.

Person   What I Learn About

_____

_____

_____

_____

_____

List the people you teach and what they learn from you.

Persons   What They Learn About

_____

_____

_____

_____

_____

Are the people that you learn from the same people that you teach? What contributes to that situation? Think about the growing you do in each of the relationships on your lists and the growing that you've helped foster in others. The most intense experiences with other people are those in which we grow together and learn about ourselves. These are not necessarily easy experiences, since they involve taking risks, but they help us become better people and better friends.

To summarize, our personal supporters not only respond in times of crisis, but they provide personal contacts apart from the issue-oriented contacts we have as process politicians. They provide the love and attention that change agents need to "keep on keepin' on".

RULES FOR RELATIONSHIPS

Every relationship has rules, and it is important that everyone know what the rules are and that they can be discussed and understood. Imagine playing a game of cards without talking about the rules and coming to agreement!

We have looked carefully at relationships to find out what makes them work and what tears them apart. We have especially taken time to talk about how we have worked on this book, developing rules for a healthy relationship between the two of us as co-authors.

We suggest building strong support groups as the foundation for healthy interactions, by observing the following rules. (They can be considered alongside the "rules to live by" that pertain to individual health, described in Chapter 2.)

BE HONEST WITH YOURSELF AND WITH OTHERS.

It is important to talk about what's happening in a relationship. If there are tensions in the air, ignoring the situation is not likely to make it go away. If something bothers us, we lay it out and deal openly with the discomfort. Likewise, if something makes us feel excited or happy, we try to share those positives feelings. This applies to one-to-one situations as well as in dealings with groups.

Eileen's relationship with the chairperson of her community group has its ups and downs. They have philosophical disagreements that must be talked about honestly. They may not come to agreement, but they try to understand one another's beliefs and feelings.

Sam is pleased with the way that he and his partner have set up their consulting business. They have taken careful steps to ensure that they compliment each other as they work. They build in positive rewards for themselves from their relationship. This positive tone enables them to work through trouble spots from a sound foundation.

In the context of being honest about feelings, it is helpful to use "I" statements to express yourself. For example, *"I felt* angry after the meeting because some issues were not resolved" is a statement that invites positive discussion. On the other hand, a statement such as, *"You really made me angry* when you left things unresolved" sounds like an attack and is likely to shut off discussion or provoke defensive arguing.

Pay attention during discussions to the nature of the exchanges. See if you can pick up cues that trigger defensive responses and those that invite resolution. Look at your responses to the phrases other people use to raise issues or discuss differences of opinion with you.

Ask your friends about how *they* see you deal with your feelings. Ask them if it is hard to approach you about touchy subjects. Taking this risk can open up the relationship and help you to learn about yourself!

It is helpful to use behavior descriptions when expressing or working through feelings. Saying, "When you do _____, I feel _____," helps the other person or group get a handle on what you are talking about.

At a meeting of City Council members and community residents, a leader from the community complimented the Council for inviting residents to the discussion.

The statement, "When you invited me here, I felt flattered and determined to do my best to have a fruitful session" gave others positive energy and allowed the community leader to share good feelings. It also encouraged positive responses and mutual efforts to have a worthwhile meeting.

Being honest with yourself does not always mean telling people exactly what you think of them or their ideas. It does mean expressing *your* opinions or feelings clearly and tactfully. If we deal with negative feelings when they're just a "pinch," those pinches are less likely to develop into a "crunch" that is debilitating. Working together to resolve conflict can bring people closer. *Not resolving conflicts can cause severe problems and split people up.*

ASK FOR WHAT YOU WANT.

This rule is more complicated than it appears. *Asking* for what you want necessitates *deciding* what you want, *examining* the implications of that decision, and *taking the risk* of not getting it. Unless you lay your cards on the table and share your dreams about how you would like things to be, the chances of realizing those dreams are slim.

This rule applies on a personal as well as a group level. Think about a group of friends who are trying to decide how to spend the evening. The group could sit around for hours, while everyone says, "I don't care; I'll do whatever other people want to do." In reality, it's pretty unlikely that people don't have preferences. Unless I *say* what I want to do, the chances are slim that the group will end up doing that.

Ask for what you want; don't expect others to guess correctly. If I want you to scratch my back but wait for you to think of it, I am not helping the relationship at all. You might not think of it, and I could end up resenting your lack of thoughtfulness. What a waste of energy!

On a group or community level, as in personal situations, it's important for members to ask for what they want. Individual group members have relationships with the group in much the same way as two individuals relate to each other. Group goals are incorporated into by-laws or resolutions; personal goals or wants within that group context must be addressed directly also.

The goals of Eileen's community organization are to build neighborhood identity and strengthen the ability of neighborhood residents to influence their own lives. Within that framework, Eileen would like to see activities and projects that get people together informally to have fun and to get to know each other. She talks with the group and asks them to respond to her request by scheduling a community rummage sale within the next month.

HELP! I NEED SOMEBODY!

Being a process politician can become a strain on anyone. Sometimes, it seems that there will never be enough hours in the day to finish all that needs doing, and sometimes we get impatient with the slowness of bureaucratic or democratic machinery.

We all go through ups and downs and have times when we're on the ball and times when nothing goes right. Unfortunately, though, the demands on a process politician do not take personal fluctuations into account.

A community leader, Bob, is going through some difficult times. He is often torn between whether to spend his time at home with his wife and family or whether to stick by his commitment to the neighborhood.

We encourage honesty in responding to situations like the one mentioned above. If people are aware that Bob is under some stress in his personal life, they are better able to be sympathetic and understanding. It's unnecessary to go into all the details, but it does help to clue people in on your life situation.

Asking for and giving help during rough times is what support groups are there for. Be sure to draw on the resources of your support people when you feel like your own strengths are low. None of us can be on top of things all of the time. We need our co-workers, friends, and an occasional vacation to keep things in perspective so that we can accomplish our goals.

———————————

References for Chapter 4:

Carl Rogers, *On Becoming a Person* (Boston: Houghton Mifflin Company, 1961).

Abraham Maslow, *Toward a Psychology of Being* (New York: D. Van Nostrand Company, 1962).

GROUP EFFECTIVENESS

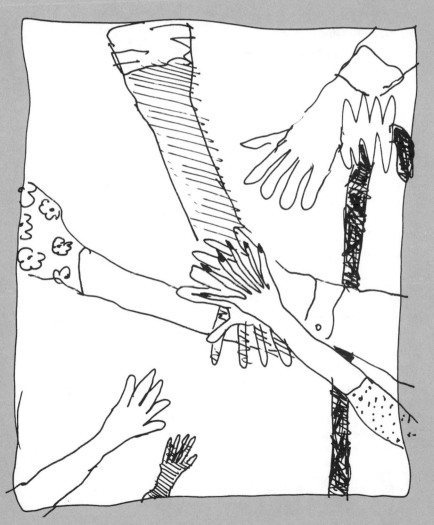

Observing how change takes place through formal and informal action in groups can give a broader understanding of how community and social change occurs as well. Part 2 presents a variety of practical suggestions for helping groups be effective, whatever the issue. These ideas emphasize broad sharing of opinions and encourage a lot of people to take part.

Chapter 5 presents some theoretical models from which to view group functioning and some suggestions about how to do periodic check-ups of your group's decision-making style and member satisfaction.

Chapter 6 introduces a step-by-step approach to planning your group's actions, beginning with identifying a focus and moving through how to set objectives and evaluate progress. The basic outline is applicable to any issue and is designed to help groups plan for success.

Chapter 7 identifies specific ways to facilitate a group's decision-making process. These concepts and tools are designed primarily to promote active involvement by all group members and decisions that will be carried out.

Chapter 8 acknowledges the informal activities that always are part of a group's life. Without behind-the-scenes conversations and thought, group decision-making could take forever.

Chapter 9 is about conflict. The subject of conflict is viewed from a positive perspective, since without diversity of opinion, a group would not be very interesting. A framework is provided for conflict management, with some basic steps for resolution into constructive results.

Active people commonly have experiences of feeling stuck, of not knowing how to be effective. Chapter 10 suggests ways to figure out what to do when you feel stuck.

The real test of a group's effectiveness lies in its ability to influence other groups and collections of groups. Chapter 11 discusses institutional values as a key to understanding social change in larger contexts.

CHAPTER 5.

HOW GROUPS OPERATE

Groups, like individuals, are growing beings. They experience childhood, adolescence, and adulthood, complete with the emotional pains and joys of each phase.

What is a group? *In process politics, we understand a group to be a collection of people who choose to interact around their common needs.* Group members share certain values and self-interests and work together to achieve their shared goals. Groups also include sub-groups, each of which has a life of its own. Groups include people who are working out their relationship to the group and to each of the sub-groups.

The term "group" is more specific than the term "community". Both are composed of people with things in common. The distinction is that group members take action in relation to their shared concerns, while a community does not necessarily do anything at all about the fact that they have a common problem.

It is helpful to have a basic understanding of the principles of group dynamics so that we can better appreciate the struggles that a group has over leadership or changing membership. A knowledge of how groups work enables us to look objectively at a group's experience and celebrate its progress.

Think back to the last meeting that you attended. How would you rate your overall satisfaction with that experience?

The key point of this chapter is that groups can be observed and managed. Knowledge of group development and group process is essential background information that helps process politicians assess what is happening and how to make things happen better. Group dynamics is fascinating to learn about especially since we are so directly affected by groups around us and the decisions that they make.

The basic principle of how groups operate is that they have both *task* and *maintenance* dimensions. Group members need to pay attention to accomplishing goals at the same time as they concern themselves with how the members are interacting. A group that focuses too heavily on tasks can have internal dissatisfaction, while a group that concentrates only on interpersonal relationships may end up getting nothing else accomplished. Process politicians try to balance task and maintenance concerns.

A group's growth and development take place both during and between meetings. Phone calls between monthly sessions, for example, are bound to have some effect on the group's task and/or maintenance components. Regardless of the content of the conversations, relationships outside the group have a bearing on the group.

All of us experience being group members, beginning with our own family unit. We expect to get something from group membership, and if we don't get it, we drop out or perhaps sabotage the group in some way.

> Think about the groups that you belong to and what
> you expect to get out of each involvement. Then, think
> about what you are actually getting.

It is important to remember that groups are all composed of individuals with needs and interests of their own. These personal agendas call for as much attention as the group's shared needs and interests if it is to be a healthy group.

PHASES OF GROUP DEVELOPMENT

No two groups are identical. They vary as much as the individuals who compose them. Conversely, all groups are similar.

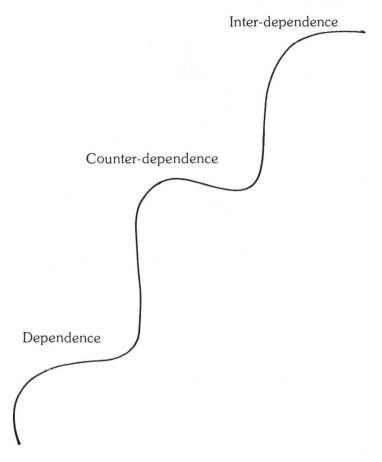

Inter-dependence

Counter-dependence

Dependence

They all go through growth phases that have predictable characteristics.

These phases parallel the phases of human development: *dependence, counter-dependence,* and *inter-dependence.*[1] It is easiest to observe these phases in a group whose membership is steady over time; it is more difficult to distinguish the phases in groups with constantly shifting membership or goals.

During the "dependent" phase, group members depend on the leaders for direction and guidance. They are not yet sure why

---

[1]Warren Bennis, *Changing Organizations,* (New York: McGraw Hill, Inc., 1966).

they are there, what they can contribute, or what roles they will take within the group. They may assume tasks at the request of the chairperson but not question that authority. The issue that people are most concerned with during this phase is inclusion: How do I fit into this group? Am I a part? This can be called the "childhood" stage of group development.

Soon, however, the group starts to encounter some bumps. There might be a power struggle, or a sub-group may attempt to railroad a decision. In any case, the designated leader's authority is no longer accepted. This represents the "counter-dependent"

phase, where group members begin to assert themselves in the form of conflict with those in the leadership roles. The issue here is influence: Who is most influential in this group? How can I become more influential than I have been? This is the "adolescent" stage of group development.

"Inter-dependence," where members and leaders work together in the process of decision-making is the mature phase of group development. It may take weeks or even years for a group with consistent membership to reach this phase; and sometimes a group never gets there. Inter-dependence is characterized by open communication, accomplishments that the entire group

feels proud of, and successful recognition and management of conflict. The issues during this phase involve communications and individual differences: Do all the people in this group count? Has everyone had a chance to express an opinion?

Development is difficult to monitor in many community groups since membership changes frequently and there are always new issues to wrestle with. Nevertheless, it is possible to observe each of the phases with regard to a given issue.

A community planning council has been working on legislation to increase tenants' rights. Within the past six months, they have successfully worked through their dependence on the chairperson and are now functioning with a sub-committee that works independently and brings recommendations back to the full group for discussion. The group demonstrates its "inter-dependent" phase on this issue.

On the issue of future highway construction through the neighborhood, the initiative rests with the steering committee. They schedule guest speakers and lead discussions at meetings of the full planning council. On the topic of highways, the group is still at the "dependent" phase.

The personal development of individual members in relation to the group is another indicator of how a group is functioning.

Susan has begun to speak out at meetings—in opposition to members who have been around for a much longer time. Until now, she was more of a listener than an initiator. She has entered the "counter-dependent" phase in relation to the group and is now investing more of herself. She has made a commitment to participate more fully.

As one member is experiencing counter-dependence and trying to oppose the leader, another may be relying on that leader for instruction. A leader should recognize the diverse needs of individual members and of the group-as-a-whole. The leader can also help the group be aware of these dynamics by talking with them about their own growth phases.

A fundamental responsibility of process politicians is to help groups grow and see the phases of their own development.

Sam and Eileen discuss a group with a member they run into outside of the formal meeting situation. During one-to-one contacts, it's easy to share personal perceptions. These contacts also build trust between process politicians and group members.

In order to figure out where a group is going, it's essential to look at where the group is in relation to both task and maintenance functions within each of the developmental stages.

For example, the process politician can point out that, as a group moves through counter-dependence, the rebellion may *not* primarily be a personality issue with the leader but a phenomenon directed at the *role* of leader. It is helpful for leaders to keep this in mind, too!

TOOLS FOR GROUP SELF-AWARENESS

It is essential for individuals to know who they are in order to grow. It is also important for groups to take time for periodic self-examination. This enables members to identify what they like

about their own operation and what needs improvement. There are a variety of facets that can be looked at, and there are some tools that can be used to help groups get a handle on each of those facets of working together.

Making use of a "fair witness" is appropriate here, with either an outside person or a relatively disinterested group member serving as impartial observer for all or part of the group's meetings.

A chemical dependency program regularly invites a process observer to sit in on executive committee meetings. This "fair witness" has the specific assignment of watching the interactions among group members. Observations are shared with the committee before adjournment, with discussion about how the group could improve.

A process observation guide can be used by the fair witness as an aid in watching for particular group behaviors and for giving feedback to group members. (See Figure 1.)

A group can decide for itself how to use the observations offered by the fair witness and may ask for suggestions also. If the discussion has been primarily among three members of the group, for instance, the fair witness may speculate that other people need additional background knowledge in order to participate more fully. Or the fair witness could suggest that the group talk about participation to determine whether they would like to change or maintain the present pattern.

Another tool to use in diagnosing a group's health is called a "maintenance check". A sample maintenance check is in Figure 2; others are included in the appendix. A maintenance check can be viewed as a diagnostic check for a group, as a medical check-up picks up danger signs in time to prevent anything more serious. A maximum of 30 minutes is required for a group to do a maintenance check; we suggest that groups use this format on a regular basis. Each member of the group takes 10 minutes to fill out the questionnaire, followed by a sharing of responses and total group discussion. The questionnaires focus on various group functions and can help figure out what phase of development the group is in.

FIGURE 1.
PROCESS OBSERVATION REPORT FORM[1]

Group _____ Date _____

Interpersonal Communication Skills
  1. Expressing (verbal and nonverbal)

  2. Listening

  3. Responding

Communication Pattern

  4. Directionality (one-to-one, one-to-group, all through a
     leader)

  5. Content (cognitive, affective)

Leadership
  6. Major roles (record names of participant)

      _____ Information-processor   _____ Follower

      _____ Coordinator   _____ Blocker

      _____ Evaluator   _____ Recognition-seeker

      _____ Harmonizer   _____ Dominator

      _____ Gatekeeper   _____ Avoider

  7. Leadership style

      _____ Democratic   _____ Autocratic   _____ Laissez-faire

---

[1]Reproduced from: J. William Pfeiffer and John E. Jones (Eds) *A Handbook of Structured Experiences for Human Relations Training,* Volume I (Revised) (La Jolla, California: University Associates, 1974). Used with permission.

8. Response to leadership style

____ Eager participation ____ Low commitment ____ Resisting

____ Lack of enthusiasm ____ Holding back

Climate
9. Feeling tone of the meeting

10. Cohesiveness

Goals
11. Explicitness

12. Commitment to agreed-upon goals

Situational Variables
13. Group size

14. Time limit

15. Physical facilities

Group Development
16. State of Development

17. Rate of development

Observer Reaction
18. Feelings experienced during the observation

19. Feelings "here and now"

20. Hunches, speculations, and ideas about the process observed

Figure 2. MAINTENANCE CHECK: FEELINGS[1]

Step 1.   Each group member reads over the following list of questions.

1. What are acceptable and unacceptable ways of expressing different kinds of feelings in this group?
2. Are there any kinds of feelings for which there are no acceptable means of expression?
3. Do people trust each other?
4. What are the characteristic ways that less acceptable feelings show themselves and how obstructive are they?
5. How much variance in individual styles of expressing feelings is tolerated?
6. How spontaneous, open, and direct are expressions of feelings?
7. Is the importance of the expression of feelings accepted?

Step 2.   Take 10 minutes for your group to discuss the following topic: In what ways have I seen some of these concerns raised in my experience in *this* group?

Step 3.   Each group member fills out the following questionnaire.

1. The way I express myself in this group is acceptable.

1	2	3	4	5
/Never	/	/	/	Always/

2. There are some feelings I have trouble sharing in this group.

1	2	3	4	5
/Seldom	/	/	/	Often/

3. I feel trusted in this group.

1	2	3	4	5
/Never	/	/	/	Always/

---

[1]From a set of "Maintenance Checks" developed by David Goodlow for use at the Regional Training Center in Minneapolis, Minnesota in 1972. They are drawn from materials developed in part by the Northwest Regional Educational Laboratory in Portland, Oregon. Reprinted by permission.

4. I feel that unacceptable feelings in this group are obstructive.

1	2	3	4	5
/Seldom/		/	/	Often/

5. I am open and direct when expressing my feelings in this group.

1	2	3	4	5
/Never	/	/	/	Always/

6. I feel that the acceptance of expression of feelings is important in this group.

1	2	3	4	5
/Never	/	/	/	Always/

Step 4.   Record the results of all members' questionnaires on a grid form posted for all to see. Spend 15 minutes discussing the group results, helping each other clarify and understand.

Some groups use self-evaluation methods that combine personal interviews, written questionnaires, and group discussion. Others call in a consultant from outside to develop assessment tools specifically geared to that group and the type of work they do. Our point is that no matter what format a group uses, *it is essential for group members to talk about how they are working together.*

After a group has critically examined its operating styles, it can define its process goals. A group that can answer the questions, "Who are we?" and "How do we function?" is then ready for the next questions: "What do we want to be?" and "How do we want to function?"

A university class determined that they functioned in a shared-leadership style, with responsibility for leading discussions rotated among class participants and the faculty. They have had regular attendance from all but 3 students and active discussion from approximately half the group.

The class decided they were comfortable with their informal style and with the sharing of leadership responsibilities. They were not happy about the uneven par-

ticipation and made a commitment to consciously encourage everyone to express opinions. The faculty
agreed to contact the 3 students who had been missing
class to welcome their return and to find out if anything
specific to the class's functioning was keeping them
away.

We encourage that decisions about how decisions are made
take place in a full group setting. We don't advocate any particular method, though; each group needs to evaluate the style
that works best for them.

It may be useful for a group to define its participation expectations through process observation or maintenance checks.

A board of directors were surveyed about whether they
preferred to make decisions quickly or with maximum
opportunity for discussion. The group agreed that it
was important to consider all members' questions or
opinions before coming to final votes. By articulating
this group value to the board, participation increased
since then everyone knew that other people wanted to
hear from them.

A group that welcomes new members by telling them that there
is group agreement on the importance of asking questions and
speaking starts the new members off with some idea of what is expected.

Another result of examining a group's interactions can be some
decisions about the group's long-range or short-term goals. It is
surprising how often groups can continue meeting without ever
taking time to be sure that everyone shares an understanding of
why the meetings take place. Many insights can happen when a
group begins defining and clarifying what they are about and how
they choose to operate.

SOME PRINCIPLES ABOUT . . .

ROLES

Within every group, individual members are needed to per-
form specific functions. Someone has to take responsibility for

bringing up new issues, for sending out meeting announcements, and for providing background information when requested.

In group dynamics literature, roles are talked about in relation to either *task* or *maintenance* functions. Task-related roles include actions that help the group accomplish things; maintenance-related roles deal with group members' participation.

A list of commonly identified roles and their definitions follows. Task roles include:

Initiator: Proposes tasks, goals, or actions; defines group problems; suggests a procedure.

Information seeker: Asks for factual clarification; requests facts pertinent to the discussion.

Opinion-seeker: Asks for a clarification of the values pertinent to the topic under discussion; questions values involved in alternative suggestions.

Informer: Offers facts; gives expression of feelings; gives an opinion.

Clarifier: Interprets ideas or suggestions; defines terms; clarifies issues before the group; clears up confusion.

Summarizer: Pulls together related ideas; restates suggestions; offers a decision or conclusion for the group to consider.

Reality tester: Makes a critical analysis of an idea; tests an idea against some data to see if the idea would work.

Orienter: Defines the position of the group with respect to its goals; points to departures from agreed-upon directions or goals; raises questions about the direction which the group discussion is taking.

Follower: Goes along with movement of group; passively accepts ideas of others; serves as audience in group discussion and decision.

Maintenance roles include:

Harmonizer: Attempts to reconcile disagreements; reduces tension; gets people to explore differences.

Gatekeeper: Helps to keep communications channels open; facilitates the participation of others; suggests procedures that permit sharing remarks.

Consensus Taker: Asks to see if the group is nearing a decision; sends up a trial balloon to test a possible solution.

Encourager: Is friendly, warm, and responsive to others; indicates by facial expression or remark the acceptance of others' contributions.

Compromiser: Offers a compromise which yields status when his own idea is involved in a conflict; modifies in the interest of group cohesion or growth.

Standard setter: Expresses standards for the group to attempt to achieve; applies standards in evaluating the quality of a group process.[1]

All of the above-listed roles are needed for a smoothly-functioning, effective group. They may be performed by separate individuals or shared by group members at different points. A fair witness can watch a group meeting and give feedback on which roles are operating; or a group can spend time discussing which roles come easiest to them and which they need to build into their group.

If, for instance, a group does not include someone who assumes the role of "summarizer," then it's helpful to assign someone to that role or to remind members to speak up when they feel a summary is needed.

The staff of a social service agency heard feedback from a process observer about their task and maintenance roles. Several roles were shared by all the group members, including initiator, information-seeker, and compromiser. No one encouraged participation by quiet members. The group decided to be more conscious to fill the gatekeeper role.

---

[1]Reproduced by special permission from "What to Observe in a Group," *Reading Book* by Cyril R. Mill and Lawrence C. Porter, Editors, pp. 28-30. Copyright 1976, NTL Institute for Applied Behavioral Science.

There are dysfunctional roles, too. Behaviors such as dominating, blocking, seeking recognition, avoiding issues, being aggressive, or distracting are disruptive to a group. It's not easy to confront someone about dysfunctional behavior, but it's important not to ignore obvious disruptors. Remember the suggestion from Chapter 4 about using "I" statements to express yourself.

A member of a community planning group monopolizes the discussion, and the other group members tune him out. The chairperson deals with the situation by saying, "I'm eager to get back to the issue that's on the table now. Would you like to request any specific action from the group at this time, Jon?" That usually enables the group to return to business.

Group members share responsibility for dealing with disruptive members. Statements such as, "I'd like to hear what others have to say" can tone down some members so that diverse opinions can be heard and discussed. Discretion is advised on whether to confront someone in public or in private. Personal attacks are non-productive, whereas sharing personal reactions can be helpful to the whole group.

LEADERSHIP

When group members identify the leader of their group, they usually name the person in the formal leadership position. If they look more broadly at influence and respect within the group, additional names come up.

A leader is any group participant who helps the group achieve its goals. It is not how many ideas a person generates or how loudly these ideas are expressed that is important. Rather, the key is how well those ideas help focus the group's energy toward the goal.

Just as we talked about formal and informal power, we can talk about formal and informal leadership. Some of the most influential people in any group are people without any official title, and some of the people with titles exert very little influence. The concept of leadership hinges on interpersonal relationships within the group. As relationships change, as issues change, so does leadership.

A useful model for thinking about leadership is a continuum between "laissez-faire" and "autocratic" styles.[1]

Laissez-faire . . . . Autocratic

The term "laissez-faire" means non-interference, or letting others do as they please. A laissez-faire leadership style emphasizes individuality and resists structuring the group to focus on task or maintenance functions. Whether intentionally or by default, laissez-faire leaders encourage group members to do whatever they are into.

> Susan was elected chairperson but felt unsure of herself as a group leader. As a result, she hesitated to assert herself to avoid doing anything wrong. The group spent much time chatting with each other, and little was accomplished. Members began dropping out.

In contrast, the autocratic leader forces the group to get the job done, whether it is working on task or maintenance goals. The autocratic leader considers open participation to be inefficient and only permits comments related to the tasks at hand. Members' feeling are unimportant and irrelevant, in the eyes of an autocratic leader.

> John called the meeting to order. The secretary reviewed the minutes, and a vote was called for. John asked the next person on the agenda to present her committee's recommendation. The recommendation was given in the form of a motion, and the vote was taken. No "irrelevant" remarks were permitted; John would immediately rule them out of order. Members went home feeling frustrated and not listened to. They had many unanswered questions about what went on.

We believe that both styles of leadership are useful and that a "good leader" combines both styles. This middle-ground is called the "democratic" style of leadership.

Laissez-faire . . . DEMOCRATIC . . . Autocratic

---

[1]From "An Experimental Study of Leadership and Group Life," by Ronald Lippitt and Ralph K. White, published in *Readings in Social Psychology* by Henry Holt and Company, Inc. Copyright 1958 by Ronald Lippitt and Ralph K. White. Reprinted with permission.

While we believe the democratic style works best, certain circumstances may call for more hard-nosed or more easy-going styles. A forceful style gets action; but a group can benefit from struggling to find direction, and that benefit is lost with an autocratic style. There is no "right" style of leadership; what is right is what helps the group achieve its goals, one at a time.

There are tools and exercises that groups can use to analyse their leadership needs and styles. We encourage groups to talk about leadership and find ways to increase the leadership skills of members. (See reference list at the end of this chapter.)

Some groups function without a designated leader; they may rotate that function, or they may deny the need for having a leader at all. We maintain that every group has leadership, whether officially designated or not. Certain people exert more influence on group decisions than others, and, unless that fact is recognized, a group that tries to function as a collective may be operating with blinders on.

How can you become a better leader? We suggest becoming familiar with the roles identified earlier in this chapter. To be an effective leader, you must be able to function in a variety of roles as task and maintenance needs unfold. Your personal support group can help you work on new roles.

DECISION-MAKING

Process politicians help people be effective decision-makers. What constitutes a "good-decision"?

1. Decisions that get carried out.
2. Decisions that take both facts and feelings into account.
3. Decisions that are understood.
4. Decisions that take self-interest principles into consideration.
5. Decisions with input from those to be affected.
6. Decisions with few harmful consequences.
7. Decisions that make sense.

How can a group reach good decisions? Some groups operate most satisfactorily by using *Robert's Rules of Order*. Others combine majority vote and free-flowing group discussion. In some, the formal leadership makes decisions for others to implement, while others make decisions by consensus.

The important thing here is for the group to consciously decide how to decide. Unless there is open discussion about how comfortable members are with parliamentary procedure, for instance, they may never get a chance to voice their confusion or preference for more loosely-structured discussion. There are no fixed rules about how decisions have to be made; the final choice is up to the group.

We are most comfortable in small groups with decision-making by consensus. *We define consensus as decision-making that takes all members' personal opinions into account and that results in a decision that all members can live with. They may not be totally happy with the outcome, but they have agreed that they can abide by it and feel their opinions were listened to seriously.*

Large groups have difficulty obtaining consensus without professional facilitation. Techniques to ensure full participation in a large-group setting range from allowing time for small-group caucusing to allowing each member to express a personal viewpoint that takes no more than one minute.

The process politician can call attention to the options for reaching a particular decision, suggesting that the decision be: (1) tabled, (2) divided into parts, (3) handled by committee and brought back in the form of a recommendation, or (4) left unresolved for the time being. The process politician can also remind the group to consider the nature of the decision and what approach would be most helpful in this particular situation.

Whatever approach is taken, encouraging the group to evaluate its results and decision-making styles is always a good idea, both as a preventive measure and to remedy problems.

CONFLICTS

Our basic belief about conflict is that it is a sign of being alive. Groups that argue stand a better chance of being able to come to good decisions than groups who disagree with what's happening but keep opinions to themselves. The leadership can solicit dissenting views and support the ideas of members as they work through both issues and process-oriented conflicts.

How each of us responds to conflict depends on the situation and on our personality. The important thing to remember is that conflict can be managed, resolved, and learned from—as further developed in Chapter 9.

MOTIVATION

People often ask, "How can I motivate our group?" The question of motivation is a question of self-interest. People are "motivated" when they are getting what they want from a given situation. On the other hand, when people drop out, it often means they're not getting what they expected.

The process politician helps people identify what their personal self-interest is in regard to a particular group. And the process politician tries to help both individuals and groups get what they want. The secret is helping people to accept the idea that personal rewards are allowed, and then helping them go after their own pay-offs.

Many fascinating developments happen in a group's life. Doing regular maintenance checks is essential to group effectiveness, in much the same way as self-awareness and feedback are essential to the individual. This on-going monitoring process becomes even more important in looking at the interactions among groups, discussed in Chapter 11.

References for Chapter 5:

Warren Bennis, *Changing Organizations* (New York: McGraw-Hill, Inc., 1966).

R. R. Blake and J. S. Mouton, *Corporate Excellence Through Grid Organization Development* (Houston: Gulf Publishing Company, 1968).

R. Lippit, J. Watson, and B. Westley, *The Dynamics of Planned Change* (New York: Harcourt, Brace, & World, 1958).

Robert's Rules of Order.

CHAPTER 6.

ACTION PLANNING AND EVALUATION

Process politics helps to manage change by developing steps for achieving long-range goals. Learning to deal with change is important for groups since they themselves are always changing. Even those who resist change attempt to manage it in a way that suits their particular needs.

Action planning helps a group find effective solutions to agreed-upon problems. Through planning, community needs and personal philosophies can be translated into actions to which the group has a commitment. Group perceptions are shared and discussed in a way that promotes success in working together.

WHY PLAN?

Planning is being done all the time by professional planners. There is always a need for coordinated planning and impact studies in such major areas as health care, housing, and economic development. In addition, there is a great need for citizen input into these planning activities.

A process politician will look for ways to help neighborhood organizations, as well as other groups, make their concerns known to planners. This can pay off by giving neighborhood people broader perspectives on their issues and a greater interest in the planning outcomes.

At the neighborhood level, planning is done in much the same way as at city hall. Neighborhood planning usually relies on professionals to cover technical details, calling on residents' expertise about local lifestyles and community goals.

Effective planning makes it possible to get the job done in a way that helps people feel productive and successful. The planner role can be shared, assigned to one person in a group, or handled by staff. Planners function like cheerleaders, helping a group applaud when it has achieved an objective, however small. They do this by working with groups to develop action plans.

An action plan becomes a road map for a group or organization to follow as it moves from where it is to where it wants to go. An action plan that is useful is one with flexibility for detours en route, stopping places for maintenance work, and realistic goals. Action planning makes it easy for a group to identify its successes and failures and to learn from them.

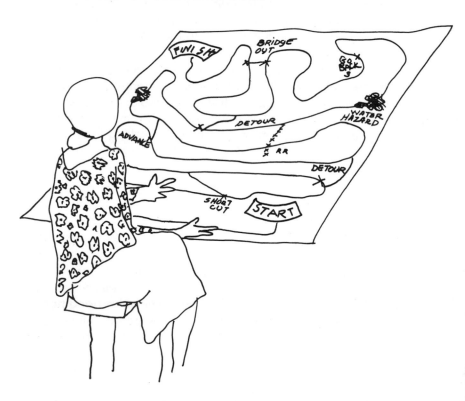

STEP 1. DETERMINING YOUR GROUP'S FOCUS

The first step in planning for action is to focus a group's energy. This may have been done prior to the group's first meeting, but if there is no clear direction for the group when it first meets, it is necessary for that group to establish its reason for being.

Almost any group can list more concerns than it has resources to work with; so it is important to limit the group's scope. One way to help your group do this is to have each member list priorities for the group.

A newly-formed advisory board had its first meeting. The chairperson started out by sharing some of his interests in being involved with this new group. He then invited each person in the room, including spectators and staff, to offer their thoughts on the direction the group could take during the coming year. The result was a long list, that included everyone's ideas.

After you have a list of individual concerns, the group members can look for areas of agreement and select general priority themes for action.

It is helpful to think about Step 1 in the action planning process as the process of deciding the name of your organization. You should also consider whether it will be a multi-purpose group dealing with a variety of neighborhood concerns. Will it work exclusively on certain identified problems? Will it be city-wide in scope? It is not necessary to be specific at this time about just what you will spend your efforts on; rather, the idea is to reach a group decision about the general subject that you want to work with.

STEP 2. DETERMINING THE COMMUNITY'S CONCERNS

Once the group has identified its priorities, they can go to the community for help in identifying specific concerns in relation to that general subject. This involves making contact with individuals, groups, or organizations to see what is already being done to deal with your group's prime focus. If your planning group is representative of the community, it is likely that their perceptions will not be very different from the community's, but it is important to check out this assumption to be sure the planning is done with an accurate understanding of community sentiment.

The decision has been made that your group will concentrate on dealing with concerns of renters in the neighborhood. Many of your group members are renters themselves and are personally aware of the difficulties in dealing with absentee owners and discriminatory rental policies. They sit down together and divide up the responsibilities for getting a more complete assessment of renters' concerns, by contacting community organizers, tenant rights groups, and individuals who are not in the group.

There are different ways to listen to the community regarding your general priority. One way is to publicly announce that there will be a neighborhood meeting to discuss all ideas related to the issue at hand, If, for instance, your priority is community spirit, you will get some good ideas if you just ask people what they think about the current level of community spirit and what, if anything, they think could be done to raise that level.

Remember: Even if every idea or concern you hear has already been mentioned during your group meetings, the person you are listening to from the community doesn't know that. He or she has taken time to think about your questions and deserves appreciation for sharing his or her thoughts. A response such as, "Yes, we already thought of that and it doesn't work" serves as nothing but a wet blanket.

Another way to get an idea about the neighborhood's opinions is to have each person in your group talk to five other people who are not group members. You could also ask people to fill out a questionnaire. In some instances, it is easier to get responses by asking questions face-to-face, rather than using a written format. In general, a simple survey with one or two specific questions will be more productive than a complicated form with many questions.

A community mental health center had a booth at a neighborhood fair. They did a survey of neighborhood residents by giving a "penny for your thoughts." Each

person who filled out the colorful sheet of paper and stated what other people in the neighborhood seemed most bothered by got a penny. The result was a thorough (although unscientific) random sample survey.

Sometimes, a more elaborate survey is necessary. A poll of scientifically-selected people will give more dependable, representative information about a community's opinions but is difficult and expensive to compute. Many communities have professional pollsters who can do this, and government planners can be called on as well. Previous studies of community issues and opinions, political parties and candidates, or university departments may also be helpful in doing a needs assessment. Students can do basic research and polling in the neighborhood in return for credit.

To get information about community attitudes, you should use a variety of data collected from a variety of sources—including information from groups or agencies who may not support your efforts.

A state agency started its needs assessment by visiting a sampling of communities in the state. They visited with various people and listened to their perceptions. In the process of listening, the staff gathered names of key individuals and organizations who were important to contact. The needs assessment proceeded by contacting each of those key people for their comments and advice.

The results of a needs assessment is that your group can develop a broad understanding of the problems they want to work on, what barriers to anticipate, and a general direction for the group to take. The next step is to develop a problem statement.

STEP 3. WRITING YOUR PROBLEM STATEMENT

While this step of the action planning process is probably the most difficult, it is also the more important! A good problem statement grows naturally out of the needs assessment process from Step 2. It summarizes the concerns that have been expressed by the community, identifies particular symptoms, and provides a starting point for moving towards solutions.

A good problem statement is specific. It deals with one issue only. If several problems are to be dealt with, several problem statements are needed. Ineffective planning stems from unclear statements about the problem with which the group is dealing.

Unclear problem statement: Members of our community group are frustrated.

The problem statement above may be true, but it doesn't say very much about the precise nature of the problem. Who is frustrated: all members or just a certain few? What are they frustrated about? What is the result of their frustration? When does their frustration occur? Who is bothered by the frustration?

Without answers to questions like these, group members can find themselves working at cross-purposes several months down the road. It may seem a nuisance to spend time over words when you want to be solving the problem at hand; but until all members share an understanding of just what you are dealing with, you could end up wasting time.

The process politician can help a group develop problem statements. Asking questions in the following format can be valuable:

1. What is the nature of the problem?
2. Who is affected?
3. What is causing the problem?

While there might be other aspects of the problem, the above format can be a beginning. To get this information, use a general discussion, a questionnaire, or individual contacts.

Once the group has analyzed its general statement in more specific terms, it becomes easier to see the many aspects of the problem. It is now possible to write a meaningful problem statement.

> Clear problem statement: Over the past several months, some members have felt frustrated with the internal mechanics of meetings. Long-time members are tired of having to repeat things for people who do not attend regularly. New members are confused about the group's purpose and do not feel a part of the group's decisions. Members are uncomfortable with the absence of group discussion before decisions are made.

Developing a problem statement is difficult work, but once it has been done it is possible to develop goals with relevance to the group's primary focus.

STEP 4. DEVELOPING GROUP GOALS

Problem statements describe a situation as it is. Goals describe a situation as we would like it to be.

Problem statement:	I'm tired of the cold winter.
Goal:	To go to Florida next month.
Problem statement:	There is always garbage in our alley.
Goal:	To work out a way to keep it clean.

Problem statement:	Absentee landlords are not making repairs on their buildings.
Goal:	To get the buildings brought up to code.

Getting from the problem statement to the goal is easy if the statement is clearly written. It is important to involve the total group in coming up with the goal. This builds group commitment to follow-through later.

> Betty agreed to take responsibility for helping her group with its goals. The problem identified by the group was the absence of activities for teens, despite the repeated requests for such activities by both teenagers and parents.
>
> At a meeting of the full group, there was open discussion addressing the problem. It was decided that the group would sponsor two evening events during the year and three weekend events to be developed with the assistance of interested teens.

The goal provides a specific direction for the group but does not include every detail for how to achieve the goal. It establishes a time guideline, the quantity of activity, and the potential participants. Yet, within those guidelines, there is considerable flexibility.

A goal is a statement of a desired outcome. Good goal statements are:

clear. The group members understand what the goal says and can explain it to other people.

acceptable to group members. Not only do group members understand what the goal says but they support the statement and will work to achieve the desired results.

flexible. The goal is not so rigid that it cannot be modified as new developments occur either within the group itself or in the surrounding environment.

long-range. A useful goal statement describes the end-point of a group's efforts. It provides a sense of direction without locking the group into specific action steps.

measureable. It contains quantifiable elements that enable the group to gauge its success or failure. If a group falls short of its goals, are those goals unrealistic, or are outside forces interfering with achievement?

Goals can be applied both to task and maintenance functions. A group could establish a goal to increase the level of participation at meetings over the next three months. Or a group could draft a proposed ordinance to submit to the city. Both types of goals are important in building cohesive, active groups.

STEP 5. SETTING OBJECTIVES: YOUR ACTION STEPS

Once a group has agreed upon its goals, it is ready to work with objectives. *We define objectives as statements of results that are achievable in short amounts of time.* They are the building blocks that enable a group to move toward its goals. The terms "strategy" or "action step" mean the same as "objective". Check out people's definition to be sure you are using a common vocabulary!

Brainstorming can be very helpful in beginning to set objectives.

Sam got together the people who were interested in taking a trip. He wrote the goal statement, "We are going at the end of next month" on a large sheet of paper as a reminder to the group. He then asked people to write up everything they needed to do to accomplish the goal. Anything was considered legitimate at this stage.

Brainstorming has one major purpose: To generate many different ideas in a short time. Creativity should be encouraged, and no discussion of individual ideas is permitted until all have had a chance to express themselves. The process politician can remind members of the purposes of brainstorming and ask people to hold off evaluating or grouping items until the brainstorm is completed.

The list of what needed to be done before the trip included many different items. Some were funny, most were very practical, others were puzzling and required further explanation.

The next step in coming up with objectives is to go over the list so that everyone understands each item. The process politician can keep people on track and ask that questions be delayed. It's important for the group to reach a consensus over which items are most relevant to achieving the goal. Any items which would not help in achieving the goal can be scratched at this point.

The list of "things to be done" ended up like this:

1. Have each person state the amount they can afford to spend on the trip.
2. Figure out approximately the cost of the trip.
3. Find out whether the traveling companions want to make stops along the way.
4. Get the van tuned up.
5. Get some extra travelers lined up in case anyone in the original group has to cancel.
6. Figure out what people should bring to cut down on the costs of food and lodging.

The objectives were arranged in priority order, someone was assigned to each task, and a deadline date for each activity was established by a few members of the group who had time to continue working. Sam agreed to be the contact person.

Sometimes, coming up with group objectives is a long process. Goal and problem statements may be complex and may present several courses of action to be followed. There are no magic formulas for dealing with such complexities, so we encourage open discussion when working toward a compromise solution. Give consideration to the feasibility of proposed action steps. Will the energy required to do the task yield comparable results in the end? Will the proposed objectives *really* help accomplish the goal? Will group members invest their time in the project? No action can work unless people are willing to take responsibility for seeing it through. Personal commitments are needed, with back-up help offered.

Good objectives state:

what will be done. The more precise an objective is, the more everyone understands what to expect and what the outcome will look like.

when it will be done. A time deadline is a good accountability mechanism and provides a framework for the responsible group member.

who will do it. At least one person should be connected with each objective. Getting volunteers may be preferable, but otherwise the chairperson should ask a particular person to take on the responsibility.

back-up resources available. This includes some discussion about where to find additional information.

Community leaders often end up carrying the bulk of the load for their group. By developing objectives that are of manageable

size, members can divide the load more readily. A "group project" that is handled by only one or two members doesn't really represent a group effort at all.

When members feel their opinions are worthwhile and welcome, the group objectives will get implemented.

STEP 6. ASSESSING GROUP PROGRESS

Groups, like individuals, need to stop and look at what they are all about. By examining what we have done, how we feel about it, and what things have changed, we learn about our work with communities and groups.

The process of translating experience into something learned is called evaluation. *We define evaluation as the assessment of how goals and objectives were implemented and the effectiveness of those processes.* When a group's planning results in clear goals and specific objectives, then evaluation can be easy.

"Evaluation" is a term that sounds complicated and boring. We see evaluation as a way of life rather than a series of charts and chi-square calculations. To evaluate means that we pay attention to questions like this:

How do we feel about what happened?
What did happen?
Why did the meeting go so well? Poorly?
How satisfied am I with the work we do?
What did we learn?
Why do I feel anxious about the next meeting?

The key in evaluation is to talk about what is happening. Once a group knows how its members feel about how things are going, it can decide what it wants to do next. If no change is called for from the originally-adopted goals and objectives, the group can then implement their action plan!

Evaluation happens both formally and informally. It happens when a group discusses its own decision-making processes, when a process observer shares observations, or when there is a structured discussion about how the group is progressing. The outcome from an evaluation process is learning about what went right, what went wrong, and how to proceed from there.

It is okay to modify original action plans. Conditions change, people you thought you could count on turn out to be "fair weather friends," and estimates of available funds may have been wrong. Evaluation gives everyone a chance to revise plans to reflect new information or changing community environments.

In planning the trip, evaluation saved the group some energy:

PROBLEM⟩objective . ⟩ objective . ⟩objective . . . . . ⟩GOAL

| | 1 | 2 | 3 | |
| "We're tired of this cold winter." | Find out how much each person can spend. | Find out how much the trip will cost. | Decide who and what to stop and see. | Get to the destination. |

That was the original summary of our action plan.

We found that the four people making the trip could spend a total of $225 on gas and travel expenses (Objective 1), and that a direct route would cost $220 (Objective 2). That left us with $5 to spend on side trips and longer routes, which greatly limited the leeway we had in dealing with Objective 3. We knew we had to revise our original action plan so that it was more realistic.

There were a number of ways to do that revision. We could get another person to go along, we could get help in covering some of the expenses, or we could decide to take the direct route. The solution in this case was to add a couple of new objectives:

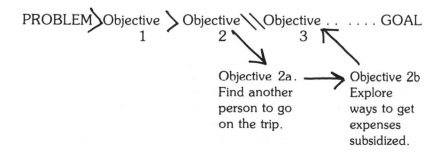

PROBLEM⟩Objective ⟩ Objective ⟩⟩Objective . . . . . . GOAL

| | 1 | 2 | 3 | |

Objective 2a. ⟶ Objective 2b
Find another   Explore
person to go   ways to get
on the trip.   expenses
                 subsidized.

The goal remained the same in this instance, but sometimes it might be appropriate to alter the goal to be more in line with new information. Sometimes, it's necessary to give up entirely on a goal. If things don't work out as was expected, it's alright for the group to scrap their original plans.

> A neighborhood group tried to get a welcome wagon project launched. Everyone was enthusiastic during discussions, but nothing visible happened. It was difficult to pinpoint the reasons for the inaction; but finally the group decided it was better to acknowledge the demise of that project than to continue to beat a dead horse.

A RAP ON APATHY

"Apathy" is a word that is heard frequently when people get together to discuss problems. It is a concern of groups who must deal with a lack of enthusiasm or interest about the group's projects.

Apathetic reactions can occur for different reasons. Perhaps the individual group member feels excluded by the rest of the group. The whole group could feel overwhelmed by the big job ahead of them and give up rather than acknowledge their feelings of helplessness. Sometimes, apathy is the result of some external problem and is not connected with the group.

It is helpful for the leadership to take responsibility for dealing with group apathy when it occurs. It is probably best to approach individuals in private about this concern; it may be easier for them to talk honestly, and they may respond to the personal attention and caring that such contact implies. Bringing up the subject of apathy in a group discussion doesn't work too well; groups usually feel blamed and do not easily open up when confronted with their own negative behavior and lack of responsiveness.

A way to prevent the onset of apathy in the first place is by stressing positive happenings within the group's life. Acknowledge and congratulate each other when things go well. Let individuals know that their contributions, no matter how small, are important and appreciated. Celebrate group successes on a regular basis to build the group's awareness of their effectiveness.

In most cases, the leadership needs to take initial responsibility for recognizing success points during a group's history. Later, other group members will pick up on that and give each other positive reinforcement more spontaneously. When this is done on a regular basis, you will have a strong, high-energy group.

Recognizing and acknowledging personal successes of individual group members is part of the larger group self-evaluation process. What makes a group effective in managing change is when the short-term objectives contribute toward achieving long-range goals—and when the people responsible for those accomplishments are recognized and thanked.

Each year at the annual meeting, awards are made to group members who made significant contributions of time, energy, or expertise to the group. An article describing the event and mentioning the recipients of awards by name is printed in the neighborhood newspaper, with photographs of each recipient included. Most recipients request extra copies of the paper so that they can send the article to friends and relatives.

An end-of-the-year celebration can help groups formally recognize their efforts, but such recognition should not wait for the end of the year. People need to feel needed. They need to have a sense of their own value within a group, and they need to feel that they have contributed toward accomplishing group goals. Helping members identify and meet their personal self-interest needs within a community action group is essential in order to avoid indifference, and support and encouragement from the leadership in regular doses can make the difference between apathy and enthusiasm.

Action planning can take many forms, and you can usually tell how well a group's planning process works by noticing the levels of energy and involvement among its members. Setting goals and celebrating achievements enable group members to learn useful skills while improving their communities and reaping personal satisfaction.

References for Chapter 6:

Chris Argyris, *Intervention Theory and Method* (Reading, Mass.: Addison-Wesley Publishing Co., Inc., 1970).

Warren Bennis, *Changing Organizations* (New York: McGraw-Hill, 1966).

Warren Bennis, Kenneth Benne, and R. Chin, *The Planning of Change* (New York: Holt, Rinehart, and Winston, 1969).

Hornstein, Benedict, Burke, Lewicki, and Hornstein, *Strategies for Social Change* (New York: Macmillan, Inc., 1970).

CHAPTER 7.

TOOLS FOR A SUCCESSFUL MEETING

Much of our work takes place in meetings, some of which are productive and some of which seem to be a waste of time. The fact that some meetings are successful and some are not could be accidental; but there are techniques to ensure success and minimize the chance of wasting time.

What is a successful meeting? We asked people how they would judge a meeting and came up with the following list. A successful meeting is a meeting where:

- People leave feeling satisfied.
- People leave looking forward to the next meeting.
- Everyone agrees that something got done.
- Lots of people came and on time.
- People stayed until the end.
- Decisions are understood.
- There is discussion of both facts and feelings about issues.
- People have an opportunity to use their skills and to develop new ones.
- Conflicts are dealt with and not avoided.
- Rewards are handed out during the meeting, as, for example, when a person is thanked for a job well done.

Add any other criteria you would use. The list above just represents a sampling of responses. The point is that success can be defined by the group itself.

DECIDING HOW TO DECIDE

One of the keys to successful meetings is to talk about the group's decision-making processes regularly. In Chapter 5 the primary theme was that any decision-making approach is okay as long as it works. Many groups decide that Robert's Rules of Order are the best way to run their meetings. We like to be more flexible with groups—calling for informal discussion and decisions-by-consensus if the group prefers that style. The point is to discuss the group's operating style, rather than automatically sliding into a particular mode.

Some groups protest when the idea of "deciding how to decide" comes up. They aren't quite sure how to handle such a discussion, or else they do not want to take time away from the more important agenda items. We believe that discussing processes is essential; no group has time *not* to deal with these concerns!

How can a group know what process to use in what circumstances? There are no absolute answers to a question like that. The choice depends on a combination of subject matter, dynamics of the issue under discussion, and the preferences of the group itself. If the leader asks the group what style they prefer, the group can arrive at its own best answer.

There are occasions when a group decides not to make a decision, and the issue is settled by default.

A community planning group was considering whether or not to admit business persons who were not residents of the community as voting members. There were two distinct factions within the group, both equally vociferous and both equally sure of their own position. The group decided not to act; any motions that came up were defeated, and the item was eventually tabled indefinitely.

The inaction of the group in the above situation left the status quo intact; no new voting members were admitted to the group.

Other indicators that a group does not want to make a decision occur when members physically or mentally "tune out." This can be observed by watching the group's body language; members may start whispering, get up and leave, or postpone an issue on the pretext that there is not enough information available.

As evident above, deciding not to decide can happen for both active and passive reasons. The important thing is to make the decision-not-to-decide a conscious one; otherwise, the group is left with no closure on that issue.

A FEW WORDS ABOUT ROLES

The task and maintenance roles within a group need not be static. The summarizer role, for instance, may be carried by four different people within one specific meeting. Or responsibility for keeping the group to its agreed-upon agenda could be delegated to a different person at each meeting.

Most groups have someone to chair the meeting (called president, convenor, chairperson), someone to take minutes (called secretary, recording scribe, recorder), and someone to oversee money matters (called the treasurer or finance person). The job descriptions for each position vary considerably, and it is important for the group to reach agreement about what is expected from each officer. It is best to agree to the responsibilities for each position before the positions are filled.

An unwritten rule is that the presiding officer acts primarily as a moderator, rather than a lobbyist, to encourage people to speak out, to present issues, and to facilitate full discussion.

A group chairperson consistently presented her viewpoint and asked the group for their endorsement. Opposing viewpoints were cut off, and general discussion was not allowed. The level of frustration among group members was high. Most people dropped out before the committee's work was done.

A group member can be designated communicator, to keep in touch with the membership and relay concerns, questions, or issues back to the full group. The communicator listens to the pulse of the group as a whole, diagnosing trouble spots early and seeking remedies before a major crisis develops.

A city-wide group was elected to deal with technical funding responsibilities. The communicator regularly called members, helped them understand what was going on, and relayed their requests for orientation and training to the full group. Without this kind of behind-the-scenes support, many of those members would have resigned out of confusion.

It is important that the communicator be cautious about exerting undue influence on committee members. The communicator's role is to relay information, *not* interpret or advocate on the basis of that information.

Another role is that of process observer who, with explicit sanction of the group, observes how the group is working and tells the group what he/she sees.

The other roles, listed in Chapter 5, can be shared and rotated freely within the group. Specific roles can be delegated if the group feels a special need, or individual members can choose different roles for their own growth. The various roles can help the group move more effectively. A facilitator can identify specific roles and invite a group to use them when that group is having trouble.

BASIC COMMUNICATION SKILLS

There has been considerable attention among human relations specialists, psychologists, personal growth groups, and others to the importance of developing good "communication skills." Most of us grew up knowing that there are four primary ways to communicate: reading, writing, speaking, and listening. That's still true, but communication skills specialists emphasize specific techniques for improving our abilities to effectively communicate.

The basic problem when people have trouble communicating is that the message *intended* is different from the message *received*. The result can be a misunderstanding or a breakdown in communications between the two affected parties. This applies to all forms of communication: verbal (the words we use), non-verbal (body language and gestures), and symbolic (how we dress or wear our hair).

The following diagram represents a summary of what happens when two people, A and B, try to communicate:

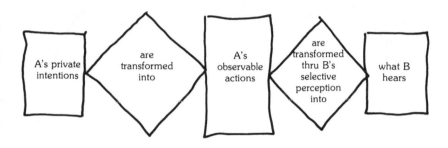

The diagram is adapted from a paper entitled "The Interpersonal Gap," prepared by John Wallen of the Northwest Regional Educational Laboratory in 1967.

Virginia Satir, a well-known figure in the human potential movement, has developed a simple way to look at our communications patterns. Her system is described below.[1]

In any situation where two or more people are interacting, there are three important components: *ME, YOU* (one or many), and the *CONTEXT* (the issue and/or substance of the interaction). Effective communication takes all three into account. Statements that suggest that *I* count, *you* count, and the *situation* counts make for congruent communicating.

---

[1]Virginia Satir, *Peoplemaking.* (Palo Alto, California: Science and Behavior Books, 1972). This material is an adaptation of her work, used with permission.

Congruent communication can be represented like this:

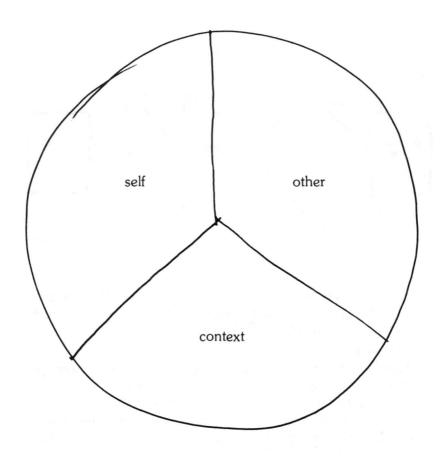

When one of the elements is left out, the communication is garbled and dysfunctional. For example, the responses to a situation where two people are dealing with a broken flower vase could look like any one of the following styles.

The *blamer* style operates in a manner that says, "I count, you don't count." The blamer might respond to the situation by pointing a finger at the other person and saying, "It's all your fault the vase broke" or "If it weren't for you, everything would be fine."

The *placater* style discounts the self and says, "I don't count, you count." The placater might get a woeful expression on his or her face, accompanied by such words as, "I'll never do that again," or "I always mess things up."

The *computer* disregards both self and others, saying "It's not the people that is the issue; it's the situation." The rationalist might respond to the flower vase situation by saying, "Let's not get excited. Let's all sit down and calmly figure out what can be done."

The *distracter* style ignores all three components of effective communication by saying, "I don't count, you don't count, and the situation doesn't count." The avoider might make a joke about the situation and suggest that everyone go out for an ice cream sundae.

Some people get into dysfunctional communication styles with particular relationships or groups. To evaluate the effectiveness of your communication style, tape a meeting or a conversation that you are part of, and then listen to the tape with a friend. Assign each statement you make to one of the above styles. You can then determine what changes, if any, you want to work on.

There are preventive measures to protect against communications breakdowns. The basic techniques have been developed by various members of the human potential movement, beginning with the National Training Lab in the late 1940's.

John Wallen developed the following categories for outlining the four basic skills for improving interpersonal communications:

Paraphrase: (concern with ideas and suggestions) Letting the other know what meaning his statements evoke in you, for the purpose of acknowledging and checking for accuracy.

"Do you mean . . . (statement) . . .?"
"Is this . . . (statement) . . . an accurate understanding of your idea?"
"Would this be an example of what you mean (giving a specific example)?"

Perception check: (concern with the person and his/her feelings) Describing what you perceive the other feels—tentatively and without evaluating him or her.

"I get the impression you'd rather not talk about this. Is that so?"
"You were disappointed that they did not ask you?"
"You look like you felt hurt by my comment. Did you?"

Behavior description: Describing specific, observable actions of others rather than stating inferences, accusations, or generalizations about their motives, attitudes, or personality traits.

"You bumped my cup," rather than, "You never watch where you're going."

"Jim and Bill have done most of the talking and the rest of us have said very little," rather than "Jim and Bill have to always hog the spotlight."

Description of feelings: Identifying your feelings by (1) name, (2) simile, (3) action urge and conveying it as information about your inner state and not as an accusation or coercive demand against the other.

• "I felt hurt when you ignored my comment," rather than, "You're rude!"

• I feel hurt and embarrassed," rather than, "You just put me down!"

• "I'm disappointed that you forgot," rather than, "You don't care about me."

• "I'm too angry to listen to any more now," rather than, "Get the hell out!"[1]

The net effect of using the basic communications skills is to open up lines of communications, ensuring understanding and validating the remarks made by the other person. The suggested responses invite clarification and a "let's work together" relationship among the involved parties.

PREPARING FOR YOUR MEETINGS

If you expect people to come to meetings, it's important to let them know the time and place—in advance. Select a meeting time that is convenient for the membership, in a location that is incontroversial and accessible to people who rely on public transportation. Regularly scheduled meeting dates are often a good idea, so that people can plan ahead and set aside that time each week or month. If you do written meeting notices, be sure to include some idea of what's going to be discussed. A sample meeting notice is on page 130.

---

[1]From "Summary of Basic Communications Skills for Improving Interpersonal Relationships," written by John Wallen. Copyright 1972 by Northwest Regional Educational Laboratory from its publication, *Interpersonal Communications.* Reprinted by permission.

The physical arrangement of the meeting room can play a part in whether the group feels comfortable. If possible, arrange the chairs and tables so that everyone can see each other. A U-shape or a large rectangle can be effective. If there are no tables, arrange the chairs in a circle, rather than in rows, to let people know that each counts as much as the others. Check out the meeting room ahead of time so that you know whether to bring a chalkboard or any other supplies. Find out where you can get extra chairs if they are needed and if coffee or tea will be available.

For small groups, it is a good idea to meet at someone's home. This creates a friendly atmosphere where people feel free to express their ideas.

A formal meeting room atmosphere can be intimidating; but it may be appropriate if the subject matter is formal. Try various room arrangements, as a way of injecting some variety into the meeting format, and ask people which they liked best.

SETTING AN AGENDA

It is important that group members have an opportunity to be involved with developing the agenda. This gives them a stake in carrying it out and opens up the process of deciding what the

---

YOU ARE INVITED TO THE FEBRUARY MEETING OF . . .

Central Community Council

Tuesday, February 8, 1977
7:30 p.m.
1900 11th Avenue South
(Emmanuel Methodist Church)
-enter on 19th St. side-

ITEMS TO BE DISCUSSED INCLUDE:

--City Council motion to decrease housing money for our community: Do we want to take some action?

--Publicity planning for up-coming neighborhood elections: Who's going to do what, and when?

--Reports from neighborhood representatives: What is happening in our community?

--Other items that people at the meeting want to discuss or announce.

PARTICIPATION AT THE MEETINGS IS OPEN TO ALL!!! IF YOU NEED

TRANSPORTATION OR HAVE QUESTIONS, CALL EILEEN AT 874-5369.

group will work on. After the agenda is developed, the group members should be invited to make additions and deletions if they feel any are needed. A sample agenda format that we have found useful follows; it sets the tone for group involvement and gives people an idea of what to expect.

The proposed agenda can be put together in consultation with group members at a steering committee, or it can be drawn up right at the meeting. Generally, some advance planning is better so that preparation, such as preparing hand-outs, can be done. Members are more likely to come if they have an idea of what will be discussed; they also have a chance to prepare individually if they want to.

PROPOSED AGENDA
10/12/76

(1 min.)   1. Call to order.

(5 mins.)   2. Review and approval of agenda.

(5 mins.)   3. Review and approval of minutes.

(10 mins.)   4. Announcements:

--Upcoming public hearing
--Workshop schedule
--A birth announcement
--Introduction of visitors/new members
--Other ?

(30 mins.)   5. Presentation by city staff: Do we like the plans they've done for our community ?

(20 mins.)   6. Neighborhood Fair: Final organizational plans for next week. Who's doing what? What else needs to be done ?

(mins.)   7. Other ? ? ?_____

(5 mins.)   8. Critique the meeting: "I liked," "I disliked," "I learned" statements from group.

9. Adjournment

The key components of this sample agenda format are the term "proposed" (or "suggested") agenda, reviewing the agenda as an explicit agenda item, and having a spot for "other" items to be added. Posting the agenda on a wall can help focus the group's attention at the start, and they can see the items checked off as they are covered.

The time limits next to each agenda item can be considered as guidelines. If the group is involved in a heavy discussion, the chair should use discretion about whether or not to cut off the discussion. Sometimes, it's enough just to comment that the time has run out, and then someone can either suggest an extension or the discussion can be drawn together and summarized.

Setting aside time for announcements can be a casual way for the meeting to get started. New members can be introduced, visitors can be welcomed, and the tone of the meeting can be established. There is a variation about how groups feel comfortable; some prefer a casual style while others are used to formalities and save their newsy items until after the meeting. If the chairperson is not sure which style is preferred, include such a discussion as an agenda item!

BRINGING NEW MEMBERS IN

The first meeting that someone attends often sets their impressions. If someone feels welcome and a part of the group from the start, he or she is more likely to become an active participant. If possible, a pre-meeting orientation by a group member who is familiar with the work can be very valuable. Also, a formal orientation packet can be prepared to hand out to new people. Another way to help bring someone on board is to assign a "pair-partner" who sits next to the new person and explains what is going on. The pair-partner may also check with the new member after the meeting to clarify any questions and to offer informal orientation.

The initial contact with a new member is a good time to share any group norms. If the group prefers to make decisions by consensus as often as possible, it is helpful for a new person to know that. If the group has stated that all opinions are important, the

new person can be encouraged to ask questions and speak up.
All previously-adopted "rules" of the group need to be com-
municated to new people so that they know their status. Pertinent
written material, especially statements of purpose or by-laws and
incorporation documents, should be given to new members
soon. Past minutes and other records can also be made available.

KEEPING PEOPLE INTERESTED

There's nothing more frustrating than to be a member of a
group and feel like you don't understand what's going on. Many
questions never get asked because the person is afraid the question will just take up other people's time.

The chairperson can plan an active part in keeping the interest
level up by offering opportunities for people to ask questions, by
expressing a need for clarification, and by making sure that
everyone has a common knowledge base for making decisions. A
brief review of a discussion, for instance, can remind people
where the group left off, bring new visitors up to date, point out
misunderstandings, and focus the conversation in a useful direction. If someone other than the chair is willing to give that brief
review, so much the better. Spread the participation as much as
possible!

Asking open-ended questions that permit sharing of opinions
lets people know that their ideas are welcome. "Yes" or "no"
questions discourage participation.

If there are lags in the discussion, or if the energy level seems
especially low, bring that observation to the attention of the full
group. Sometimes, if the hour is late and people are tired, it's silly
to push things. Other times, people tune out because they are
afraid to express their true feelings. Offering the group an opportunity to talk about the group atmosphere often frees things up
and brings people back in.

HOW TO HELP GROUPS SHARE THEIR OPINIONS

All too often, group members leave a meeting feeling frustrated
and angry because they didn't express an opinion or because
someone monopolized the discussion. This does not have to happen, and there are some "tricks of the trade" that open a group

up and deal with monopolizers quickly. Many times, the leader is aware that particular issues will be controversial. Reviewing possible ways, prior to the meeting, for facilitating those discussions can alleviate some problems.

Process suggestions that can be proposed to a group include:

- Allowing time for each person in the room (guests included) to express a personal view, with a time limit for everyone and a right to "pass" without making a statement.

- Asking the group to think through their opinions, prior to going around the room on an equal-time basis.

- Recording opinions on the chalkboard as they are stated, reminding people not to repeat an idea once it is recorded.

- Going around the room with a "sentence completion" phrase such as, "I would vote no (or yes) on that proposal because _____," and a suggested time limit.

- Asking the group to list pros and cons to the issue, with the object of getting as much information as possible before the group.

Groups often have trouble expressing opposition to an idea that is on the floor. Some helpful statements to invite criticism and objections to what is going on are:

"Does anyone have a problem with that idea?"

"Is anyone especially uncomfortable about that?"

"Let's take some time to see if there are negative aspects to the direction we're moving in."

"Let's alternate 'pro' and 'con' points in response to this motion. Okay?"

The premise behind this is that unless people have a chance to express objections *during* decision-making, the resulting decisions will not be as sound. If someone feels they were excluded from the discussion, resentments may crop up later; and the final decision may get sabotaged in some way.

HOW TO ENCOURAGE GROUP SELF-AWARENESS

The process politician, whether in the role of chairperson, group member, or outside observer can call a group's attention to how they are working together. If there seems to be tension in the room, for instance, the process politician might say, "I'm feeling tension in the room right now, and it's getting in my way. Is anyone else aware of that feeling?"

A simple "I" statement such as that can help the group deal with its maintenance right when it's happening. By demonstrating such interventions, the process politician is in the role of "educator" and is actually teaching group process skills to the group.

Another way to support group self-awareness is by periodically evaluating how the group has been working together. This may be done by phoning all members to find out how they felt about the last meeting. Or it may be by doing a quick maintenance check (see Chapter 5) during a regular group session.

Handing out copies of a process observation guide (see Chapter 5) can also increase group members' awareness of the various aspects of group behavior. Sometimes, an individual member will voluntarily begin using the process observation sheet; other times, the whole group rates themselves as a checkpoint on their interactions.

End-of-the-meeting critique sessions are also useful self-awareness devices. Simply asking the group to call out (1) what they liked about the meeting, (2) what could have been better, and (3) how they are feeling now can give a quick reading of ways to improve the meeting. This same check-up can be done on an evaluation form, that people fill out before they go home. The important thing is to make use of this information as helpful suggestions for making people feel better about their participation and the work of the group.

HELPING MEMBERS TO "RETIRE"

No one can be expected to be a group member forever. People leave groups for a variety of reasons, many of which are legitimate and indicators of growth in the person. A resignation letter needs to be responded to personally, preferably by the group's chairperson, so that there is a private opportunity to find out whether the person is moving on for personal reasons or because of some dissatisfaction with how the group is functioning.

We like to encourage "retiring" members to personally share their decision with the group. This provides an opportunity for an exchange of feelings, including formal expressions of thanks to old-time members or suggestions about how group members might keep in touch later.

That's also a good occasion to get suggestions for future issues the group might consider, based on the expertise of the member who is leaving. The retiring member might be asked to suggest someone who could be invited to join, so that there are no gaps in the membership.

HOW TO TERMINATE A GROUP

Sometimes, the best thing that can happen to a group is for it to dissolve. That's why establishing measureable, specific tasks to be accomplished is important; once the job is done, the group can break up.

It's also okay for a group to take a recess from time to time. If there has been consistently low participation and low energy among the members, that could be an indication that people are doing other things right now and this group is not a top priority for them (such as around Christmas time). Rather than fight that, it might be wise to acknowledge the group's feelings and make alternate plans. Cancelling a meeting and having a potluck dinner instead might provide just the change of pace that's needed, besides giving people a chance for informal contact.

If a group's job has ended officially, or if the group's term of office has expired, it helps to deal directly with group members' feelings about that. A celebration of some kind, where group members get to formally recognize the termination of their group, is important if the group is to leave with a feeling of completion. Members might want to exchange addresses, arrange to get together again in the near future, or just say goodbye in a way that's comfortable.

Making a conscious decision that a group to which you belong is no longer effective and should be dissolved is difficult, but sometimes that's best. If the decision was the right one, people are bound to feel relieved and freed up to pursue other interests.

Whether a group chooses to operate with a highly-structured or more flexible style, it is important to be familiar with some of the techniques that can be used to ensure successful meetings. This knowledge is applicable in any group setting, can enhance group life, and encourages broad participation.

References for Chapter 7:

Leland Bradford, *Making Meetings Work* (La Jolla: University Associates, 1977).

Virginia Satir, *Conjoint Family Therapy* (Palo Alto, Calif: Science and Behavior Books, 1967).

Virginia Satir, *People Making* (Palo Alto, Calif: Science and Behavior Books, 1972).

CHAPTER 8.

BEHIND THE SCENES: WHERE THE ACTION IS

Almost everything that goes into group decision-making can happen *outside* the meeting format, except formal ratification of decisions. Groups go on even when they are not in formal session.

Good process politicians acknowledge the importance of activities and interactions that happen outside the formal decision-making processes; they recognize that any outside interaction, whether task or process oriented, is part of the group's development. Informal contacts between group members are, in many cases, more economical (in terms of time, energy, etc.) for some functions than within the group's formal meetings.

Community groups that deal with complex systems and institutional structures need behind-the-scenes contacts. Not everything can be done within the confines of a meeting. People need time to get to know each other. They need a chance to think through their personal and group goals, and they need to do the background work or information seeking that precedes decision-making.

Think about a group in which you are an active member. List the kinds of contacts you have with group members—behind the scenes. Who initiated the contact? What was the content? What was the result?

How many of the contacts were instances in which someone was asking for advice? How many were just occasions for sharing personal frustrations or feelings about what went on at the last meeting? How many were oriented toward planning for the future? How many of the contacts could have a bearing on the way the group works together, either positively or negatively?

It's important to be aware of what happens between meetings and to know how to use those situations most productively.

EXTRA-GROUP DYNAMICS

We discussed earlier the dynamics of group development and how groups grow from dependent into inter-dependent bodies. This kind of growth takes place during formal meetings, as well as outside the meeting room.

We believe that at least 75% of the work that groups are involved in can take place outside the formal decision-making process. Many decisions get made well in advance of the final vote, whether we choose to operate in that manner or not. Anyone who wants to be influential in a community needs to remember that much of the action takes place behind the scenes.

This is not a bad thing; behind-the-scenes action is simply a fact of life. Without behind-the-scenes action, many meetings would be a waste of time.

Some typical activities that happen in-between meetings are:

- The chairperson contacts members for ideas about the next meeting's agenda.
- A new member requests an information session with a committee person.
- John and Jim arrange to have lunch together.
- Betty goes to find out about other groups who are working on issues that her group is concerned about.
- The committee secretary types up and mails out the minutes.
- A citizen lobbyist calls legislators to urge them to support a particular bill.

The term "extra-group dynamics" describes activities relevant to a group's growth and progress which take place outside the formal meetings. The concept of extra-group dynamics emphasizes that groups do not stop developing once the meeting is adjourned. Struggles and growing pains get dealt with behind-the-scenes, and the group starts its subsequent meeting with additional activity that rarely shows up in the minutes.

The board meeting was held with the head table looking out over rows of folding chairs. Three days after the meeting, the chairperson got a phone call from a relatively new member who wanted to know why such a formal seating arrangement had been used. The new member recommended that a less formal style be used, with chairs in a casual circle and all members facing one another.

The next meeting was arranged with chairs in a circle. The new member worked through personal issues with the group by initiating this change, and he was now a contributing member of the total board.

As a rule, we find it useful for a group member to plan to spend an equal amount of time outside meetings as in the meeting room. Pre-meeting meetings, for instance, often help prepare for an issue so that the discussion flows smoothly and all aspects of the issues are sure to come up. This does not mean that solutions should be brought in to the group as finished proposals; that would be contrary to all that we believe in as process-oriented activists. Planning is for determining *how* to handle a specific issue and for thinking about long-range goals and how to accomplish them.

The community planning council decided to spend their next meeting discussing subsidized housing. Since this is a broad topic, the officers spent several hours contacting members to find out what was of interest to them. They gathered resources and invited technical people to be at the meeting. They also put together a suggested agenda for the meeting. No specific expectations were decided ahead of time; the pre-meeting activities were to plan the process for facilitating discussion.

What is the process politician's role in extra-group activities? In many ways, the extra-group arena is where the process politician is more active.

It was the process politician who first called attention to the fact that a number of group members were frustrated with the way that meetings were being conducted. John, as chair, had no idea that people found his style was threatening. The process politician suggested that John solicit feedback from members over the telephone. John did that, and group satisfaction and productivity went way up after a group discussion about how best to go about making decisions.

The process politician can help the group leadership keep in touch with the pulse of the group. The process politician has a responsibility to bring group concerns to the attention of the leaders and to suggest ways to deal with those concerns, much as an ombudsperson whose "cause" is healthy group functioning.

BEHIND-THE-SCENES ACTIVITIES

A variety of activities can happen in between formal meetings. These can be either task or maintenance activities and also some logistical functions. Some require extensive time, and other can happen in brief telephone encounters. Some of the task-oriented activities include:

- Working with staff to figure out who will take responsibility for what
- Leafletting the community with meeting announcements
- Developing a strategy for dealing with the latest City Hall maneuvers
- Doing research on a politician's voting record
- Reaching out to new groups in the community to invite participation in your group
- Touching base with group members to get their ideas for the next meeting's agenda
- Checking out rumors
- Seeking advice from respected persons in the community
- Lobbying for things the group believes in
- Following through on assignments delegated at the last meeting

The activities listed above deal with getting things done that are relevant to the goals of an organization. The second type of behind-the-scenes activitiy has to do with group membership and interactions that can pull the group together or tear it apart. These activities may not have a direct bearing toward the accomplishment of group goals, but they do affect the attitudes and commitment of members who are ultimately the ones who make or break an organization. Some of these activities include:

• Checking with new members to see what their expectations are
• Going out with a potential group member to establish some personal rapport
• Unwinding after the meeting with your friends
• Reflecting privately about the events of the previous months
• Establishing contact with other group members whom you don't know very well yet
• Inviting your personal support group to a potluck dinner
• Asking for advice on how to handle a disruptive group participant
• Straightening out personal conflicts, maybe with the help of a third party
• Forming coalitions both within and outside of your system.

There are also many behind-the-scenes activities that take time and must be consciously planned for and arranged.

• Mailing out meeting announcements
• Cleaning up after a meeting and putting chairs back in place
• Keeping attendance records and reviewing them to be sure that memberships don't lapse
• Keeping the financial records up to date
• Baking cookies to be served at the meeting
• Arranging transportation for members.

The handling of the basic mechanics sets a tone that either encourages or turns off member involvement. A group that is horribly disorganized may not be able to cope with more complicated neighborhood or community issues.

Remember: All of the activities listed here are part of a group's development and history. It is helpful for most of them to happen outside of the formal group sessions. Otherwise, little would get done!

BEHIND-THE-SCENES PERSONALITIES

Think about the people you come in contact with as you deal with your organization and its projects. Are they all organization members? Are they all volunteers? What functions do they serve during your contacts with them?

Our experience has shown that many people important to a group's development never attend a meeting but provide valuable assistance nonetheless. It's helpful to think back to the roles that we identified as necessary for effective group functioning (see Chapter 5). Basically, behind-the-scenes personalities fall into those same role categories. It's just that their activities happen outside the group.

Bob, who was hired by the city to provide staff support to a community group, most frequently serves as an information-provider. He also serves as a third-party sounding board if the chairperson needs to check out ideas in-between meetings. Bob does not consider himself to be a bonafide group member, yet his behind-the-scenes involvement with group members definitely helps shape the group's growth.

Traditionally, staff play certain support roles to groups and usually try to maintain their separateness from the group with which they work. We question the idea of staff being separate from group functioning. Even though a staff person may not be a voting group member, that person can serve to promote and enrich group effectiveness. This concept ties in with the maintenance functions primarily, where the staff efforts focus on communicating members' concerns to the group.

Lately, Bob has been doing some process observation during meetings and shares his feedback with group members in between meetings. He offers his comments as food-for-thought, listens to the reactions, and later formulates suggestions about how to help things go better. These suggestions are discussed with group members informally and subsequently—if there is group support—brought before the entire group for consideration.

In this situation, the staff is in the role of "fair witness," as discussed in Chapter 2, even though the fair witness activities take place behind the scenes.

A variety of consultants contribute to group success and progress without ever attending a meeting. It's important to make use of the idea of everyone-as-consultant because people like to be asked for their opinions.

The neighborhood improvement group realized they needed some fundraising assistance. They decided to make use of their personal contacts in various fields. Each group member agreed to approach a potential "consultant," to solicit his or her professional advice about fundraising techniques. No one who was approached refused to help out; in fact, they all felt flattered to be seen as people with knowledge that could be useful to others.

Remember: Every community or group has access to unlimited resources. No organization needs to feel limited by its membership list or its budget. Feel free to call on behind-the-scenes resource people.

The more groups solicit outside assistance, the better decisions they make and the more support the group will have in the long run.

Some groups formalize the functions of resource consultants by hiring someone to provide time-limited expertise on a particular subject matter. We encourage creative use of community consultants in between meetings to enrich the group and build links to other segments of the community.

The leadership of a group or committee cannot take total responsibility for the functions that take place behind-the-scenes. What is important is to acknowledge that it is natural for people to talk about issues among themselves, with that discussion process seen as a valuable opportunity for people to learn about each other and about changing community issues.

CHAPTER 9.

THE ROLE OF CONFLICT: USING TENSION CREATIVELY

A community board decided to have a training session on conflict. The group arrived knowing only that the subject for the evening was how to deal effectively with conflict. There was obvious tension in the air; people sat silently, looked around nervously, and waited for the meeting to begin. The staff joined the group and began the session by inviting group members to share the feelings they'd had while they waited. As they responded, reasons for the group's anxiety came out: "I was afraid someone would get angry." "I didn't want to cry in front of the group." "Conflict is such a negative thing that I was afraid we might tear down some of the good things this group has."

The reactions of this group were predictable. You can count on people to be anxious about conflict, even discussions of conflict. This anxiety may be a result of fear that the conflict will destroy the group, or it may come from a desire to avoid angry feelings.

It is unfortunate that conflict has only negative connotations. As we see it, conflict is a natural result of diversity within a group that has different values, self-interests, and points of view. We believe that healthy groups encourage their members to contribute and ask for what they want. Whether in a group or a relationship, conflict is a natural condition of being alive. A group that does not experience conflict is probably not very creative, active, or strong. On the other hand, unresolved conflict can tear a group apart.

Groups experience conflicts of various types:

- Disagreements over what problems the group should be working on
- Differences about how to accomplish goals the group has established
- Feelings of rejection that a group leader picks up
- Confusion about whose opinions are most valued

The role of the process politician is to help a group acknowledge and deal with conflicts as they arise, to *manage the conflict*. Unless conflict is managed in some way, it will produce random or haphazard changes.

With effective management, conflict situations can be turned into change that advances the group's interest and health. A group that successfully tackles a tough situation emerges healthier and stronger than one that fails to recognize and work on conflict issues.

CONFLICT AS THE CONTEXT FOR CHANGE

Change and conflict go hand in hand. There is a direct correlation between the rate of change a group or community experiences and the amount of conflict that is present: the faster the change, the more conflict you can expect. The process politician helps manage change and conflict so the group moves toward its desired goals rather than away from them.

The natural tendency for a group is to resist rapid change, although even the status quo situation is not always perfectly static. The status quo is maintained by the desire of members not to rock the boat, group traditions, or members' self-interests. Some of these forces push toward the group's goal; others push away. When these forces are in balance, the status quo is maintained. As one set of forces gets noticeably stronger, change happens.

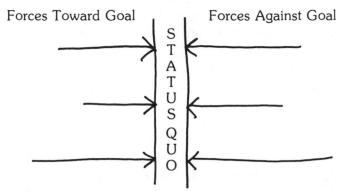

Forces Toward Goal · · · · Forces Against Goal

STATUS QUO

A conflict situation occurs when these forces are thrown out of balance. A new force comes into play, or an old force is no longer present. The status quo is jarred, and the group begins to question its position, its future, and its very existence. By the time the forces are in balance again, there could be a new status quo that is either favorable (closer to the goal) or unfavorable (farther from the goal).

Conflict changes a situation; the status quo continues it.

MAKING CONFLICT WORK FOR YOU

The key to making a conflict situation work positively is to think that it can. Remind each other of the exciting possibilities, and you will be surprised at the new ideas generated by the tension.

It is not necessary for the process politician to create artificial conflicts in a group. What the process politician needs to do is to help a group recognize conflict and help them admit it to themselves and to each other. Once you've acknowledged the presence of conflict, it's important to understand that, for a while, the group will experience it as a problem. People need time for that. But don't get stuck there longer than you have to. An experienced process politician knows when a group is ready to start working on solutions and takes action to bring that about.

Thinking about conflict as creative tension can help to break through old ways of thinking.

A neighborhood group found out that a private builder had plans to tear down several old homes and construct a hi-rise on the site. The presence of this creative tension spurred the residents toward changing zoning restrictions that would permit such activity; the resulting zoning prohibited it both on that site and in other neighborhood locations.

At times when the status quo has been disturbed, change agents need to consolidate their energy in a way that realigns the status quo. If you or your group are causing the conflict, your ability to manage it is limited; and you may have to call on an uninvolved third party to help out.

It's important to be aware of how you and your group respond to conflict. In general terms, people show either a flight or a fight response. If they possess basic skills for managing conflict, they are less likely to avoid and more willing to resolve the issue at hand.

BASIC CONFLICT RESOLUTION SKILLS

Conflict resolution occurs when the parties to the conflict understand each other's stance accurately and proceed on the basis of those agreements or disagreements. Clear communicating is the basis for managing conflicts. Too often, individuals who are arguing misinterpret each other and come to conclusions that seriously miss the mark. Review the communications skills outlined in Chapter 7, and keep in mind that miscommunication is the source of many conflicts.

The process politician can help people use their power effectively by encouraging them to seek out their personal support group members to ventilate and sort out feelings about a conflict situation.

The process politician can also help people in conflict to think in creative ways. An approach that is very useful is called the "WIN/WIN" style, as illustrated below:

You lose / I lose = LOSE / LOSE
You win / I win = WIN / LOSE
You lose / I win = LOSE / WIN
You win / I win = WIN / WIN

Approaching conflicts from the standpoint of looking for WIN/WIN results encourages people to work together for mutually beneficial solutions. The WIN/WIN approach takes into account the self-interest issues at stake and maximizes chances for everyone to get at least part of what they want. WIN/WIN shares problem-solving rather than resolving conflict through competition.

BASIC STEPS FOR CONFLICT RESOLUTION

STEP 1. RECOGNIZE THAT A CONFLICT EXISTS.

Conflict—in and of itself—is neither good nor bad. It has no inherent moral quality, and its impact depends largely on how people respond to it. While conflict is neutral, people don't respond to it neutrally. They run from it, get ready to fight, or pretend that it isn't there. Facing conflict can increase the effectiveness of a group or a relationship, and it can build intimacy and understanding.

Eileen worked with a group for several years. She felt frustrated, so she shared her frustrations and anger with the group. The resulting eruption forced new group dynamics and broke a stalemate that was uncomfortable for everyone.

Admitting to yourself that there might be a problem is the first step of conflict management. Problems can be ignored, but that doesn't make them go away. They are bound to come out some time, perhaps disguised as something else. This avoidance behavior can divert energy away from the group's goal.

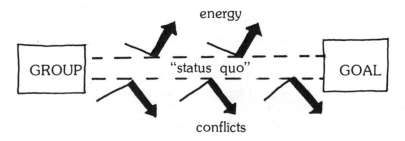

STEP 2. ACKNOWLEDGE TO THE GROUP THAT THERE IS A CONFLICT.

Before a group can begin to resolve a conflict, they must acknowledge out loud that a problem exists. No matter how it is brought up, the mention of conflict issues helps to surface other feelings that group members have been sitting on. Turmoil occurs, and the group has trouble seeing beyond the hassles raised by the conflict. They may get stuck there unless something is done fairly quickly.

Members need encouragement to express their feelings freely in response to the identification of a conflict issue. Voicing emotional reactions at this point is important in and of itself. Unless there is a chance to vent anger or resentment, the group will not be able to approach the conflict from a rational point of view, and resolution will be difficult.

STEP 3. DIAGNOSE THE CONFLICT.

To use conflict productively is to look beyond the conflict issue itself and examine the possibilities that have been created: "How can we work this out in a way that resolves the issue and also moves us toward our goals?"

It is difficult, especially when strong emotions are stirred up, for a group to move into the diagnosis phase of conflict management. That's why it is essential for the process politician to take some action right away. The process politician can contact individual group members behind-the-scenes, to provide a listening ear and also to begin exploring what is causing their emotional responses. It's also important for the process politician to help members see the possibilities for resolution if everyone agrees to work toward that.

Diagnosing conflict involves finding out as much as you can about what is happening, who is involved, and who feels the strongest. The struggle may be mainly one person's personal struggle that group members really don't understand. Or the struggle may be between two group members who are vying for power within the organization. Conflict can be between two people or between groups within the same system.

Knowing the main characters will help you understand the conflict. People with personal stakes in the conflict have trouble seeing ways to resolve it. Often, it's helpful to call on group members who do not have such a stake to be creative and think up ways to resolve the conflict successfully.

Once the people in conflict have been identified, find out what type of conflict you are dealing with. Sometimes, the disagreement is over goals:

> Randy and Pat agreed that they wanted to take a trip together this winter. Their conflict was that Pat wanted to ski and Randy wanted to go south. Their goals were in conflict.

Sometimes, people agree on goals but are in conflict over how to accomplish those goals.

> Last year, Randy and Pat decided to go to New Orleans together. Randy wanted to drive, while Pat insisted on flying. The conflict centered around how to achieve the mutually-agreed-upon goal.

Conflict results from actual or perceived differences in values, needs, styles, or interests. Such individual differences may lead to distrust among group members.

> A business association invited some community residents to their annual meeting. There was tension in the air as soon as the community people walked in. Neither group trusted each other, based on assumptions about one another's competing values.

Diagnosing conflict can take place during group discussions or outside of the meetings, depending on the issue and the group's ability to discuss it. If the group is unable or unwilling to talk, the process politician can contact individuals to share in their perceptions of the group's interactions with one another.

The neighborhood organization was unable to focus on conflict diagnosis because members still felt emotionally overwhelmed about the issue. Eileen talked privately with members and was able to get a sense of the group's diagnosis. When sharing her observations, she tried not to confuse what she was perceiving with the perceptions of group members.

STEP 4. IDENTIFY INDIVIDUAL NEEDS OR WANTS NOW THAT THE CONFLICT HAS BEEN ACKNOWLEDGED AND DIAGNOSED.

To resolve conflicts, it is important for each person who is involved to have a clear idea of what each group member wants. Ask group members to write down the main things they need to see in the final outcome to feel satisfied. Someone may need to make an explanation to the group or need to apologize about a past mistake. These need/want statements can be shared out loud or posted for others to look at. It is important for the sharing process to be non-judgmental, and time should be allowed for clarification of statements as well.

This step gets people ready for talking about solutions that can meet the group's needs. The members are now looking beyond the conflict issue itself and are thinking about conflict resolution.

Two group members said they needed an opportunity to share their opinions with the group. They wanted to feel understood although it was not important to them whether or not the other group members agreed. Another member wanted to drop the issue entirely and felt that further exploration would be fruitless. Others wanted to make an effort to find a resolution that everyone could live with.

STEP 5. IDENTIFY MUTUALLY-EXCLUSIVE NEEDS OR WANTS.

If three group members want to work on resolving the conflict and two others want to drop the whole discussion, it appears that there is a deadlock. Sometimes, a group member may personally prefer to drop the discussion but would agree to pursue it in the interest of the group. Members who clarify the degree of flexibility in their need/want statements open up new possibilities for action. However, if there are areas of complete disagreement, it's important for everyone to know that.

The process of looking for areas of disagreement can be very productive. Often, individuals see their own rigid thinking by becoming aware of a variety of perspectives. Also, the process itself becomes a group effort and can help begin to rebuild bridges.

STEP 6. IDENTIFY AREAS OF AGREEMENT.

Looking for areas where group members agree on needs and wants positively opens up the negotiation process. It may have seemed that there were no areas of agreement at all, until the group consciously looks for them. There may be resistance if the conflict is a long-standing one which has polarized group members into distinct camps. The process politician can help free up the group once they have decided that they want to work toward resolution.

A visual illustration of the group's discussion could look like this:

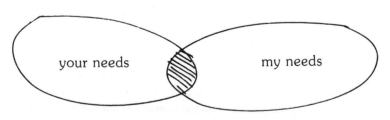

areas of agreement

When you concentrate on the agreements—the things you've got going for you—you build in success. Also, when people succeed, they find it easier to tackle the big problems. The more attention paid to the various possibilities, the less energy wasted on problems.

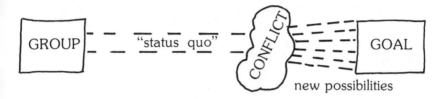

new possibilities

Sometimes, it is impossible to find areas of agreement, no matter how hard you try. You might be able to agree only that you don't want to try to work it out right now, which is still an agreement! The process politician's role is to help people be satisfied with how the conflict was approached, even if the outcome is to disband the group.

STEP 7. DEVELOP A PLAN TO ACT ON AREAS OF AGREEMENT AND DO IT.

Now that the areas of agreement have been identified, the group can begin planning its strategy for action. The result will be an action plan for resolution of the conflict. Using action planning steps (see Chapter 6) is appropriate here.

THINGS TO REMEMBER ABOUT CONFLICT

- The key to making conflict work for you is to remember that conflict, like other problems, is solvable. When you act like that is true, it tends to happen.
- Possibilities are more fun than problems—and more effective, too.
- There are more than two possibilities in most situations. The more possibilities you can think of, the better your chances of finding one that is acceptable.

• Action planning is a way to manage conflict.
• Anyone can learn to be creative and think of new possibilities. You can train yourself to be creative by brainstorming, fantasizing, daydreaming, or meditating.
• Finding overlapping self-interests usually leads to WIN/WIN solutions.
• People who take an extremist position can help surface conflict in a group and provoke positive (or negative) action.
• The important thing is not whether we have conflict but how we deal with it.

References for Chapter 9:

Blake, Shepard, and Mouton, Managing Intergroup Conflict in Industry (Houston: Gulf Publishing Co., 1964).

Jay Hall, Conflict Management Survey (Conroe, Texas: Teleometrics International, 1969).

Walton, Interpersonal Peacemaking: Confrontations and Third Party Consultation (Reading, Mass: Addison-Wesley, Inc., 1969).

CHAPTER 10.

WHAT TO DO WHEN YOU DON'T KNOW WHAT TO DO

As process politicians, we frequently find ourselves in situations where we simply don't know what to do next. These are times when all the diagnostic tools and techniques in the world seem irrelevant, and we are unable to come up with appropriate answers. Situations like these are inevitable for those who work with people, and it's important to have ways to handle them. Learning occurs at those times when you don't know what to do.

Since all problems have an infinite number of solutions, then figuring out the solutions has more to do with one's mindset than a set of techniques. Have you ever noticed, in an emergency, how people are able to do things they never dreamed they could do? Afterwards, they scarcely believe they actually did those things. This ability to get "unstuck" can be learned and put to work by process politicians.

IDENTIFYING WHEN YOU DON'T KNOW WHAT TO DO

Not knowing what to do is no real problem to the process politician; it happens all the time. You think things are going along fine when you realize that you don't know at all what is happening in the group. You feel like the cartoon character who has run off the edge of a cliff and does alright until he looks down and realizes that he is standing in mid-air. Knowing that there will be times

when you "run off the edges" can make it easier to deal with such situations when they happen and help prevent them in the first place. The first step is to be able to know when you're "stuck."

There are signals to watch for that indicate when you might be getting close to the edge of your competence. One danger sign is the fox-hole syndrome, characterized by pulling back and trying not to be noticed. We all have our fox holes, ways we avoid situations where we are not comfortable. Since we don't know what to do to change that uncomfortable situation, we retreat and concentrate on protecting ourselves from unknown consequences. We are on the defensive.

Sam worked with a business that tried to resolve problems by changing its organizational structure. They reorganized their departments every year. When one of these changes was coming up, the tendency was for the managers to hold back and take no risks until the reorganization was over.

Another sign that you may be "stuck" is when it seems like your friends are all wrong. Sometimes, we get so involved with a project that we don't see mistakes we are making. We may also have trouble listening to other people who try to point those mistakes out to us. When you become isolated from your support group and they all disagree with you, you may be painting yourself into a corner that will be hard to get out of. "Either/or" thinking may be another indication of being "stuck." When you think that if you don't do Option A, then your only alternative is Option B, you are limiting your options and may be heading for trouble.

To get your thinking freed up, you must first admit that you don't know what to do. Once you have made that admission, you become more able to put your creativity to work, ask for help, and explore new options. There is nothing wrong with not knowing what to do. It happens to everyone, and it teaches us new things about how the world works.

GETTING PREPARED FOR ACTION

It is important to remember that problems are solvable *and* that unlimited possibilities for action exist in any situation. Creative solutions can often come from people who are unfamilar with the intricacies of the issue and have an outsider's perspective.

You might decide to "opt out" temporarily if you become so wound up with the problem that you have a hard time separating yourself from it. You could take a short vacation or a leave of absence from your group in order to get some space for yourself to think. Sometimes, it is most effective to retreat formally to gain a new perspective and prepare yourself for getting "unstuck."

FIGURING OUT WHAT TO DO

Once you begin to think positively, you will find exciting new possibilities opening up to you. Even if you don't know what to do, act as if you do! It's surprising how much your attitude has to do with your ability to find creative answers to problems.

There are a number of specific ways to go about developing new strategies. Some can be done alone, and some are most effective in a support group setting. In either case, an open approach that relies on feelings, intuitive hunches, and a diversity of opinions is helpful.

> Mike demonstrated the value of involving a group in coming up with ideas. Each person first wrote a personal list of alternative actions, placing a premium on quantity. The lists were shared in the group, each person having an opportunity to share one idea at a time. The sharing continued until everyone had shared all the ideas they could think of. Some were funny, some were realistic, some were ridiculous. The group ended up with a pool of over 130 ideas to work with.

Brainstorming generates ideas from which to choose. Such a list might be developed by people sitting together or from phone contacts with individual group members. Have fun generating ideas; try using a suggestion box or polling your neighbors. The particular approach depends on the time and energy you have available.

When there is little time for figuring out what to do, there is very little time to worry and spin your wheels; this may be best anyway!

> Eileen was asked to facilitate a group meeting where there was conflict. She started off the session by letting the group know she had no plan. Together, they figured out what to do and relied on their collective intuition to work things out.

Some process politicians don't know until afterwards why they did something. Don't be afraid to act on your hunches. They're usually right!

It's helpful to write down what is going on and what needs to happen next. Writing forces you to sort out your thoughts and put together what fits with what. This is especially useful if you have not had a chance to analyze the situation carefully. When you write down what you want to say, you are able to be more articulate, especially about controversial topics.

Some other strategies that you can consider include:

- Hiring a consultant
- Getting some new people to join your efforts; you may be trying to do too much
- Going with the group on a weekend outing to clear your heads and get a fresh perspective on things
- Withdrawing from the situation by quitting the group or lowering your resistance
- Allowing the project to be a failure. Remember: People are not able to experience success unless they are free to fail.
- Getting involved with the political arena and leaving the neighborhood behind
- Reading about the experience others have had working on projects similar to yours

HOW TO AVOID GETTING "STUCK"

Learning what to do when you don't know what to do serves a dual function. Knowing that there is a way out of the "foxhole" can keep you from getting stuck there in the first place! The more you think in terms of possibilities instead of limitations, the less dead ends you run into.

The lists of what to do when you don't know what to do never ends. Once you have a grasp of the basic tools for figuring out what to do, you will be surprised to see how fast you can learn and how many solutions you can create.

References for Chapter 10:

William Glasser, *Positive Addiction* (New York: Harper & Row, Publishers, 1976).

Joseph Chilton Pearce, *Magical Child: Revolution in Mind-Brain Development* (New York: Dutton Company, 1972).

CHAPTER 11.

GROUP EFFECTIVENESS AND SOCIAL CHANGE

For process politicians who are active beyond their own neighborhood, the work becomes increasingly complex, interesting, and difficult. Sometimes, it seems as if nothing can be done to make improvements at the neighborhood level short of changing economic and political structures at all levels. Every time we get close to achieving a community goal, another roadblock appears, and our plans often need to be completely rethought.

It is important to keep in mind that groups, like people, are usually found in a larger context. A group gains effectiveness not in isolation but through interaction and influence with other groups. And, just as a group consists of individuals who join together in order to achieve a common self-interest, groups join together to be more effective in achieving their shared goals.

An awareness of the self-interest issues of the individuals and groups involved is essential if you want to be effective beyond your own group. The complexity may seem overwhelming, especially if the self-interest issues of the various groups are in direct opposition or are not acknowledged at all.

A neighbor called the block club to get a traffic light moved. A formal request was submitted to the city, signed by residents within a three-block radius of the traffic light. The request sat on various desks for almost four months, with no visible action.

The block club found that the request was held up because the Traffic Engineer's office was waiting for the city to approve additional budget money for that department. There was a deadlock, and no response to the neighborhood request was expected until that deadlock was broken.

In this illustration, there are a number of self-interests to be considered: the neighborhood resident group, the Traffic Engineering Department, and the City Council Budget Committee. Without an awareness of what is going on between and among these groups, the neighborhood people are at their mercy and will not see the traffic light changed.

SYSTEMS AND THEIR VALUES

When several groups are linked together by common concerns, values, and/or organizational structures, they form a system. *We use the term "system" to describe a collection of interacting groups that have structured their interaction in some form.* The larger a system becomes, the more compromises are needed. Personal beliefs and values get expressed less often, and individuals feel less personally involved.

As a system becomes legitimized, it takes on an identity all its own, independent of the individuals who are in leadership roles or the sub-groups which comprise it. The system itself becomes the focal point, rather than individual members' needs and self-interests.

Internal energy and resources are called upon to fulfill system goals, even when this requires individuals to act contrary to their personal values or beliefs.

A major city hospital is faced with increasing pressures from government and the insurance industry to cut costs for delivering health care. Despite personal priorities on delivering services directly to patients, supervisors within the hospital are called upon by the administration to attend meeting after meeting on fiscal management and third-party reimbursement mechanisms.

Over time, the values of a system become formalized and take on a life of their own. They become institutionalized, and the principal mission of the evolving institution becomes self-perpetuation. In an institution, individual values are, by definition, less important than institutional values—those values that maintain the system.

We use the term "institution" to mean a system which has formally-defined relationships among its interacting components and which also has a definable set of values and assumptions governing those interactions.

As a system evolves to become an institution, decision-making responsibility becomes obscured, and individuals experience a growing sense of alienation and apathy. Paperwork mounts, and documentation becomes the byword. Conformity in dress and in operating procedure is demanded more and more, with people getting ostracized or transferred out of the way if they threaten the institutional values.

These unwritten institutional values determine the priorities and the behavior of the institution, whether the values agree with the official mission statement of the organization or not. This adds a new dimension of complexity to the process of change—institutional self-interest.

The key to influencing change in institutions is to recognize when the issue involves institutional rather than personal self-interests. Here are some ways you can tell when institutional values are the issue:

1. The behavior within the system is at odds with the stated purposes of the system.
2. Despite good intentions, individuals' needs are frustrated by the system's demands for orderliness and accountability.
3. It's difficult to find out who makes decisions.
4. You hear people using words like "they" and "them" frequently, suggesting strong feelings of powerlessness about their situations, whether chosen or imposed.
5. Much of the system's resources go into maintaining information systems with a corresponding reduction in resources devoted to people.

6. There is increasing pressure to conform to prescribed dress codes and behavior patterns.
7. You hear phrases such as, "That's the way it has always been done," suggesting the influence of tradition within the system.

Making change in the context of a system or institution is an immense challenge, especially if the issue requires change in institutional values.

> As the hospital's value of cost-effective care at the expense of quality care became more widely felt among the nursing staff, morale went down and complaints from staff and patients went up. No one had any answers about how to resolve the dilemma, but everyone (including top administrators) blamed "them."

Changing institutional values requires a major commitment in time and energy by individuals throughout the system. The initial task is to find people within the system who feel that their personal needs and interests are being limited by the institution's self-interest needs. The self-interest among those individuals is the shared desire to challenge the institutional values and to get their own needs met more effectively. This common interest can form the basis for building a new power base within the system, a power base whose very presence jars the existing balance of power.

A MODEL FOR UNDERSTANDING POWER IN SYSTEMS

One way to look at how systems work is to construct a mobile to represent a system with which you are familiar, such as the city system for delivering services. At the top, there is a framework from which all the rest hangs. Each of the groups is represented by larger pieces, to which may be attached smaller parts representing sub-groups and individual members. Some groups are directly connected to the superstructure or to other groups, while other connections between components may be less apparent.

The key to a mobile is balance: The stability of one branch is dependent on the existence of stable conditions throughout. Just

as you can't add or move a piece without making an impact on the whole mobile, any change in a group has an impact on the whole system.

If there is a change in the balance of power within a system, the whole system gets out of balance. In order to regain balance, new power relationships must be identified and formalized.

The relative power of any group in a system greatly influences that group's view of issues and priorities. The Power Lab we described in Chapter 1 provides some categories that illustrate how power differences can affect an individual's or group's perception of reality.

Powerful Ins, the power elite, tend to see the system's needs in broad perspectives. Their constituency is the system itself. They tend to perceive the needs of individuals and groups as less important than the needs of the existing system. Since their power in the system is linked to the status quo, they tend to resist change in institutional values. Regardless of their motives, Powerful Ins are pulled between long-range concerns and group and individual needs. As a result, decisions take time.

Powerless Ins, the helping people, rely on their skills to exert influence. The power they have lies in their knowledge of the needs of various groups in a system. By helping groups articulate their concerns, they can strengthen the building blocks of change in the system. Systems are complex, and the temptation is strong for Powerless Ins to deal with symptoms rather than causes of problems. People's immediate needs are important, but so are the larger systemic issues that caused the needs to exist!

Powerless Outs, members of groups with no political clout, do not have access to decisions that affect them. They may be "out" by choice, by active exclusion, or by tradition. They feel excluded and take on behaviors that reinforce their powerless place in the system; they focus on immediate short-term individual issues. The feeling of powerlessness that this group experiences is real. They can see every day that they have less than other segments of their system. But they may not have the skills at hand to successfully enter into negotiations with those who do control decision-making, and they often resign themselves to a less-than-equal fate which becomes a self-fulfilling prophecy.

The Powerless Outs do have some forms of power, but unless those forms are built on and strengthened, the group will not be able to effectively use its power. The power of the Powerless Outs lies in the unifying force of their common condition. It is this unity that can be harnessed for their mutual benefit.

Saul Alinsky, author of *Rules for Radicals,* developed his community organization model by finding ways to harness the energy of the Powerless Outs to effect change. Organizers of these efforts are often members of the Powerless In group, who apply their skills to deal with the oppression of the Powerless Outs.

Powerless Outs are not just the poor or members of minority groups. Many other segments of society also perceive themselves as being powerless. Whether the lack of power is real or perceived, the feeling of powerlessness and alienation is what needs to be recognized. People who feel powerless *are* powerless unless something happens to show them otherwise.

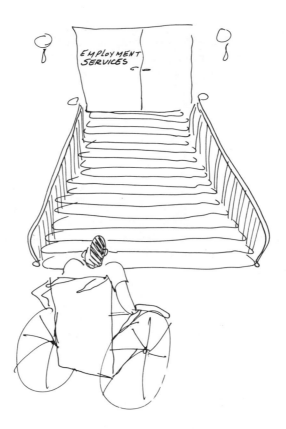

A factor that interferes with the ability of Powerless Outs to turn their situation around is the fear of losing what little they already have. They already feel victimized, and experience has shown them that it is generally safer to keep quiet. The Powerful Ins control access to survival tools (money, jobs, housing), the legal system, educational institutions, and more.

Systems, like groups, do not exist alone. Every system is connected to other systems in a wide variety of ways. The mobile we used to picture a system is really part of a larger mobile in which all the parts are intricately inter-connected.

This larger context has groups and systems with a vast array of inter-dependent institutional values and power relationships. This is the setting for long-range social change.

References for Chapter 11:

Gregory Bateson, *Steps To an Ecology of Mind*. (New York: Ballantine Books, Inc., 1975).

Louis Knowles and Kenneth Prewitt, *Institutional Racism in America*. (Englewood Cliffs, N.J.: Prentice-Hall, Inc., 1969).

Edgar H. Schein, *Organizational Psychology*. (Englewood Cliffs, N.J.: Prentice-Hall, 1965).

Note: Our sources for the Power Lab come from Sam Miller's experiences beginning in 1968. Many people have been involved in developing the Power Lab concept, including Barry Oshrey and others in the National Training Labs, Hartz Brown and others in the Metropolitan Ecumenical Training Center in Washington, D.C., and Lin Butler and Jeanette Williams at Brotherhood Pilot House in Baltimore.

EPILOGUE:

SUGGESTIONS FOR FURTHER THOUGHT

The question of how process politics approaches are applied, and in what issue areas, is not given much attention in *MAKING CHANGE*. Mostly, we believe that people need to make personal choices about that, for themselves. We would, however, like to share some thoughts about what we see as key issues and trouble spots of the future and how you can get involved.

AT THE GRASSROOTS LEVEL

We see a growing enery within and directed toward neighborhoods. People are identifying with a particular geographic community and are coming together more and more to address common interests and to meet each other. Frequently, neighborhood groups include residents, business persons, service providers, and others interested in that specific neighborhood.

Government workers, too, are being encouraged by the federal administration to expand their contacts into neighborhoods, to solicit ideas and to maintain visibility with the ultimate recipients of service.

We support this movement and we see its potential usefulness growing as neighborhood organizations begin combining their strengths to form coalitions and networks based on mutual self-interests. As process politicians, we devote considerable attention to working with neighborhood-based programs and groups to strengthen existing leadership and tap new talents.

There are neighborhood-based movements now going on in economic development, tenant rights, housing rehabilitation, energy, consumer affairs, child care, and more. If you're interested in helping to make change, these are good places to start.

ON THE JOB

Another good starting point for applying process politics is at work. A number of people from various fields are beginning to study options for how to make the most of work for both management and workers. New ideas now being given serious consideration include "flex-time" (where employees can choose to work any eight hours within a 12-hour time period), "shared positions" (where two individuals share one full-time job), and "stress avoidance training" (for managers and supervisors to learn to minimize negative effects of high-pressure jobs).

Collective and cooperative management styles are being developed all over the country—in food co-ops, feminist organizations, political action coalitions, and community development corporations. There are growing numbers of organizations using other-than-hierarchical management structures, with many on solid ground and performing much-needed community services.

Federally-funded efforts to impact the unemployment picture, such as CETA and public service programs, are bringing about some interesting situations on jobs. Service organizations which had relied totally on volunteer help have acquired paid staff virtually overnight. What at first seemed like a perfect answer to problems of overwork and unreliability sometimes turns into a headache, as the realities of government paperwork, inexperienced management, and political conditions set in. Attention is needed to figure out how to make the most of this situation.

Whether we function as internal or external change agents, the challenge of helping to develop fulfilling management and decision-making styles within a work setting is exciting. Next time you hear yourself grumble about something you don't like about your job, take initiative to get some changes made.

AT THE POLICY-MAKING LEVEL

Opportunities are increasing by leaps and bounds for consumers of services to have a say in determining the shape of those services. The movement toward maximum feasible participation of low and moderate-income people in decision-making has expanded into new fields; billions of federal dollars are now tied to requirements for citizen participation at the local level. Boards and commissions which used to consist only of "blue ribbon" names now include a cross-section of representatives from private, government, and community sectors.

Public interest groups often act as watchdogs to ensure that grassroots consumers get strong representation on advisory bodies and national study commissions. But responsibility for monitoring trends and advocating for citizen-concerns does not rest with someone else. Each of us shares that responsibility and, if we choose to take part, we can all help develop ideas for solving the problems currently facing us as a society.

If you're interested in learning about ways in which you can directly influence decisions in such fields as health care, the environment, or urban areas, an easy way to start is to contact your congressperson's office and get advice on how to proceed. As elected officials, those people are there to help the public understand how decisions get made and how we can have access to those processes. There is also a directory available through the Community Services Administration in Washington, D.C. which summarizes each federal program requiring citizen participation and what those requirements are.

Once you get involved in an advisory committee or a study commission, take initiative for getting the information, training and technical assistance you need to be effective. Insist on an orientation period that pays attention to maintenance issues (How will we run our meetings? Where can we hold our meetings to promote full participation?) as well as technical concerns (Whose job is it to implement this commission's recommendations? What are the government regulations governing Community Development Block Grant funds?). As you hear individuals express opinions about how things are going in the committee's work, encourage them to state those feelings to the rest of the group so that there is opportunity for the group to take action to avoid trouble spots and build in group self-awareness and ownership of decisions.

THE QUESTION OF ETHICS

If there is a code of ethics for process politicians, it has to do with the uses and abuses of power. Effective process politicians are powerful. They have access to information about issues and people, and they can influence who gets that information and how it gets used.

Power, in and of itself, is neither good nor bad. We all have choices to make about taking or not taking power in our own lives, and we have further choices to make about how to use that power once we have it. As we see it, appropriate uses of power are those which enhance the ability of other people to use their own power. Inappropriate uses of power keep people in dependent relationships.

It is important to establish an accountability mechanism of some type to help keep perspective and avoid misuse of power. This works in much the same way as the system of checks and balances which is set up among Congress, the President, and the judicial system. One way of monitoring your own use of power is to ask your support group and/or constituents to help you. Encourage them to let you know what they're thinking and to share any ideas they have about how to make things better. Seek out feedback from them about how they see you functioning, and listen to what they are telling you. Let people know you want their comments and criticisms as a way of helping you to stay on track.

Power can be used for the good of other people or for personal gain. It is of utmost importance for process politicians to be conscious of how they are using their power by periodically taking time to assess the impact of their behavior.

A significant barrier to effective change is greed. Greed occurs at all levels of individual functioning from the personal to the institutional, and it causes people to take action based on a very narrow and personal concept of self-interest. Process politics builds in some controls on personal greed with its value on long-range perspectives and broad-based involvement in decision-making. At the same time, it is important to remind groups frequently of their missions and of these values as a way of discouraging parochialism and encouraging WIN-WIN approaches to problem-solving.

Losing on a community issue is no justification for throwing in the towel and giving up on WIN-WIN models for change. There are bound to be times when we lose. What's important is to be able to acknowledge our efforts, identify where we went wrong, and learn from the mistakes and successes we had along the way. No matter what the outcome, the process of trying to bring about change jars the status quo, increases people's knowledge and skills, and impacts the balance of power within the system. There may be retrenching and backlash as immediate repercussions, but the learning that takes place during that process can ultimately lead to WIN-WIN solutions that will stick.

CHANGE AND NON-ORDINARY REALITY

We have defined process politics as a set of assumptions and techniques to help groups manage their own growth and development toward becoming capable, effective problem-solvers. We have discussed ways to use personal and group self-awareness to achieve concrete results and solve specific problems.

We have occasionally used terms like "energy," "intuition," "hunches," etc. These terms point to a different reality that we believe is experienced universally. It is called by names like faith, cosmic consciousness, psychic phenomena, and higher power. These words all refer to the life forces that shape the universe and transcend rational categories of thinking and acting.

While our perceptions may not always be attuned to notice spiritual forces, we believe they are always interacting with the physical realities we contact through our senses. Change in one accompanies change in the other. We think it is important to keep them working together, by asking questions like: Does what I am doing contribute to global cooperation? Does it feel morally right? Is this God's will? Does participation in this activity give people more than it takes from them?

In this book, we have applied the strategies of self-awareness and planning to the process of change primarily on the physical plane. Many of the same strategies are also applicable on the spiritual plane. The world needs more people working for change on both planes.

APPENDIX

MAINTENANCE CHECKS:[1]

The five maintenance checks which follow are adapted from those developed by David Goodlow for use at the Regional Training Center, University of Minnesota, in 1972. He used ideas from a variety of sources, including Northwest Regional Education Laboratories.

Each of these maintenance checks includes five steps and can be completed in approximately 10 minutes. We recommend that they be done in the order in which they are presented.

MAINTENANCE CHECK 1: MEMBERSHIP

Step 1. Each group member reads over the following paragraphs and reflects on the questions and his/her membership role in the group.

As we become a member of this group, we tend to concern ourselves at first with the nature of our membership. Individuals identified as being part(s) of the group are said to have membership. At the level of the individual, membership applies to issues of a person's self-identity. It speaks to questions of:

1. Who am I?
2. What can I be?
3. What do I expect and desire of myself?

---

[1]From a set of "Maintenance Checks" developed by David Goodlow for use at the Regional Training Center in Minneapolis, Minnesota in 1972. They are drawn from materials developed in part by the Northwest Regional Educational Laboratory in Portland, Oregon. Reprinted by permission.

For more complex levels of group behavior, it speaks to such questions as:

1. What does it mean to be a member of this group, organization, community, or society?
2. Will I be accepted?
3. How will I be expected to act and respond?
4. What norms will prevail?
5. Will I be trusted?
6. Will I feel satisfied that I am needed and respected?
7. Will I feel adequate?
8. Will my personal motivations fit in with those of the group?
9. How much freedom will I have to express myself?

Step 2. Discuss in your group the following topic. Try to stay on the topic as closely as possible; everyone should attempt to help the group stay with the topic.

"In what ways have I seen some of these concerns raised in my experiences in other groups (not this group)?"

Step 3. Each group member fills out the following questionnaire.

1. How clear are you about your membership role?

/1   /2   /3   /4   5/

confused   clear

2. Do you feel you are accepted on an equal basis as others in the group?

/1   /2   /3   /4   5/

unaccepted   fully accepted

3. Am I able to converse in whatever manner I am accustomed to when I am in this group?

/1   /2   /3   /4   5/

never   always

4. Do I have the freedom to express myself while in this group?

/1   /2   /3   /4   5/

never   always

5. Do I understand what this group expects of me?

/1   /2   /3   /4   5/

I do not   fully
understand   understand

6. Do I feel trusted by the others in this group?

| /1 | /2 | /3 | /4 | 5/ |

not at all   fully

7. Do I feel uncomfortable while working in this group?

| /1 | /2 | /3 | /4 | 5/ |

uncomfortable   very comfortable

8. Am I expected to give up my values, beliefs, and motivations?

| /1 | /2 | /3 | /4 | 5/ |

totally   not at all

9. Am I committed to being an effective member of this group?

| /1 | /2 | /3 | /4 | 5/ |

uncommitted   fully committed

Step 4. Record the results of the questionnaire of the group members on a grid form. Each group member will have a record of all responses. Do not discuss.

Group Member

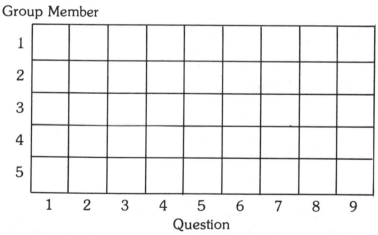

Question

Step 5. Discuss the results of the data you have now collected from your group. Do not defend your answers. Try to understand and be clear about what others and you are feeling. (All members are to try to help the group observe these guidelines.)

MAINTENANCE CHECK 2: INFLUENCE

Step 1. Each group member reads over the following paragraph and reflects on the questions and his/her influence role in the group.

As membership concerns begin to clear, questions arise in a group concerning the flow of influence between and among the group members. Influence can be defined in terms of control, manipulation, or facilitation. Control can be considered at one end of a spectrum of choice, facilitation at the other.

Control   Manipulate   Facilitate
. . . .
one choice   few choices   increased choices

Influence questions center around the manner one influences or is influenced and the member who influences or is influenced, such as:

1. Who is the leader in the group?
2. Does the leadership vary with concerns?
3. How do decisions get made?
4. Are we having "power struggles"?
5. Are we open to being influenced, or are we resisting? Are we "counter-dependent"—resisting because of a need *not* to be influenced?
6. What opportunities are there for each member to exercise leadership or influence?
7. Are there individuals in the group who care more about the power of being leaders than they do about the goals and issues of the group?
8. Is influence used by exerting the power of "experience" or "knowledge" or "emotional commitment"?
9. Are roles we bring in from outside the group used to influence the group? If we have roles that imply expertise in certain areas, is that used to control the decisions of the group?

The more we deal effectively with these influence concerns within the group, the more each member will feel committed to the group's decisions and the more effective will be the implementation of goals. Think about what problems you may have in this group concerning control, manipulation, and facilitation.

Step 2. Discuss in your group the following topic. Try to stay on the topic as closely as possible; everyone should attempt to help the group stay with the topic.

"In what ways have I seen some of these concerns raised in my experience in this group?"

Step 3. Each group member fills out the following questionnaire.

1. Do I tend to decrease or increase the choices of others by control, manipulation, or facilitation?

/1   /2   /3   /4   5/

decrease   increase
choice   choice

2. Do I feel controlled, manipulated, or facilitated by members of the group (one or more)?

/1   /2   /3   /4   5/

decrease my   restrict my   increase my
choices—   choices—   choices—
controlled   manipulated   facilitated

3. Is leadership controlled or does it vary with concerns or tasks of the group?

/1   /2   /3   /4   5/

controlled—   varied—
always the   most take leadership
same person   at different times

4. How are decisions usually made in the group?

/1   /2   /3   /4   5/

Vote—power struggles   consensus

5. Do I tend to be open to alternative solutions or do I usually have an opinion that is set at the beginning?

/1   /2   /3   /4   5/

set opinions—   open to many
difficult to change   alternatives

6. Is the group open and searching for alternatives or is it usually locked in struggles between members with set ideas?

/1   /2   /3   /4   5/

Locked into   Open to
set ideas   alternatives

7. Does the group have members who use their outside roles to unduly influence the direction of the group?

/1   /2   /3   /4   5/

Roles used   Everyone exerts
to exert undue   influence without
influence   undue reference
                                               to outside roles

Step 4. Record the results of the questionnaire of the group on a grid form. Each group member will have a record of all responses. Do not discuss.

Step 5. Discuss the results of the data you have now collected from your group. Do not defend your answers. Try to understand and be clear about what others and you are feeling. (All members are to try to help the group observe these guidelines.)

MAINTENANCE CHECK 3: FEELINGS

Step 1. Each group member reads over the following paragraphs and reflects on the questions and his/her role in this group.

Perhaps the most crucial contribution of psychology in the past few decades has been clarification of ways that feelings affect the operations of groups. They can affect any and all functions in facilitative and blocking ways. Feelings are tangible, measureable, and enduring. Feelings which are not expressed as they occur are frequently expressed later in disguised, inappropriate, and obstructive ways. Questions such as these are important:

1. What are acceptable and unacceptable ways of expressing different kinds of feelings in this group?
2. Are there any kinds of feelings for which there is no acceptable means of expression?

3. Do people trust each other?
4. What are the characteristic ways that less acceptable feelings show themselves, and how obstructive are they?
5. How much variance in individual styles of expressing feelings is tolerated?
6. How spontaneous, open, and direct are expressions of feelings?
7. Is the importance of the expression of feelings accepted?

Problems probably arise most frequently from lack of clarity about feelings. They can also stem from conflict over how feelings are expressed. Reflect on these questions and your role in this group.

Step 2. Discuss in your group the following topic. Try to stay on the topic as closely as possible; everyone should attempt to help the group stay with the topic:

"In what ways have I seen some of these concerns raised in my experience in this group?"

Step 3. Each member fills out the following questionnaire.

(See Chapter 5.)

Step 4. Record the results of the questionnaires of the group members on a grid form. Each group member will have a record of all responses. Do not discuss.

Step 5. Discuss the results of the data you have now collected from your group. Do not defend your answers. Try to understand and be clear about what others and you are feeling. (All members are to try to help the group observe these guidelines.)

MAINTENANCE CHECK 4: COMMUNICATIONS

Step 1. Each group member reads over the following paragraphs and reflects on the questions.

As a group clarifies its membership, influence, and feelings roles, it begins to concern itself with communication issues. Questions arise that deal with norms about the manner in which concerns are dealt with by the group or by individuals. Note here that information applies to things that are news. There may be other kinds of noise that are unintelligible or redundant. Such noise usually distorts, rather than aids, the passage of information. These are some of the important questions about communication.

1. Who talks to whom about what?
2. What modes and personal styles of communication are unacceptable or acceptable in the group?
3. How efficient are communications in terms of information flow versus noise and redundancy?
4. Is there feedback of information, checking for understanding, and opportunity for two-way flow where needed?
5. Are formal and informal patterns of communication primarily functional rather than bound by tradition and conflicts or limited by assumptions?
6. How do norms, roles, expectations, and feelings influence communications?
7. Are there bottlenecks, blocks, gaps, or points of overload in the lines of communication?

The patterns a group selects, as the norm for its communication, will help or hinder the group's effectiveness. Reflect on these questions and your role in the group.

Step 2. Discuss in your group the following topic. Try to stay on the topic as closely as possible; everyone should attempt to help the group stay with the topic:

"In what ways have I seen some of these concerns raised in my experience in this group?"

Step 3. Each member fills out the following questionnaire.

1. Am I able to say what I think or what I feel?

/1	/2	/3	/4	5/
never				always

2. Am I listened to by the group?

/1	/2	/3	/4	5/
never				always

3. Do I feel interrupted or cut off by others?

/1	/2	/3	/4	5/
never				always

4. Do I feel controlled by others?

/1	/2	/3	/4	5/
never				always

5. Am I blocking others so they cannot fully express themselves?

/1	/2	/3	/4	5/
never				always

6. I receive and understand feedback.

/1	/2	/3	/4	5/
never				always

7. I give feedback to others.

/1	/2	/3	/4	5/
never				always

Step 4. Record the results of the questionnaire of the group members on a grid form. Each group member will have a record of all responses. Do not discuss.

Step 5. Discuss the results of the data you have now collected from your group. Do not defend your answers. Try to understand and be clear about what others and you are feeling. (All members are to try to help the group observe these guidelines.)

MAINTENANCE CHECK 5: INDIVIDUAL DIFFERENCES

Step 1. Each group member reads over the following paragraphs and reflects on the questions and his/her role in the group.

Each member of a group represents certain unique experiences, knowledge, and skills. Few groups seem to reach a point where they take maximum advantage of these individual differences. It's rather common for members of a group to reach a level of sharing feelings where each sees the others as likable because they are pretty much the same as he/she is. This is sometimes referred to as the "honeymoon stage." If enough trust develops, the members may begin to be able to both recognize and value the individual differences that each possesses. A new set of questions then takes on meaning.

1. Do the members take the time and effort to learn about the experiences, attitudes, knowledge, values, skills, and ideologies of each other?
2. Does each work at sharing his/her own ideas in order to get others' reactions and different ways of looking at issues?
3. Do they let each other know they appreciate these differences when they don't necessarily agree with them?
4. Is appreciation of these differences merely an acceptance that there are differences rather than an attempt to find the commonalities behind those differences and a feeling of deep understanding that these differences can add to the effectiveness of the group if understood?
5. Is it important that we are different just to be different or to find one's niche by being different? Or do we look for those points of commonness where we can come together and allow the differences to create new insights and understandings about each other?

Groups have a tendency to attempt to level out these differences or to polarize around them to form power factions. As groups are able to deal with individual differences, they tend to find new resources for their effectiveness.

Step 2. Discuss in your group the following topic:

"In what ways have I seen some of these concerns raised in my experience in this group?"

Step 3. Each member fills out the following questionnaire.

1. Are feelings expressed openly so that differences become apparent in the group?

/1	/2	/3	/4	5/
no expression of feeling, or feelings expressed inappropriately			open expression of feelings—appropriate indication of what is going on inside each member	

2. Do members of the group discuss the values, beliefs, attitudes, etc. of each member?

/1   /2   /3   /4   5/

not discussed—   well known—
unknown   discussed

3. Have you shared your values, beliefs, attitudes, etc. with this group?

/1   /2   /3   /4   5/

not shared at all   shared openly

4. Do you feel "concerned" about the values, beliefs, attitudes, behavior, etc. of other group members?

/1   /2   /3   /4   5/

very "concerned"   feel appreciative
            of differences—
           not "concerned"

5. Does the group understand your uniqueness and accept you for it?

/1   /2   /3   /4   5/

does not understand   understands and
or accept   accepts

6. Do members of the group feel the commonality of each member aside from the task it has?

/1   /2   /3   /4   5/

no feeling of commonality   common areas
except for task   understood

7. Does the group attempt to influence each other to be and think alike in most respects?

/1   /2   /3   /4   5/

attempts to level   allows each to
all to think and   think and be
be alike   as they are

8. Do you feel pressure to give up what you think, believe, and do?

/1   /2   /3   /4   5/

feel much pressure   no pressure

Step 4. Record the results of the questionnaire of the group on a grid form. Each group member will have a record of all responses. Do not discuss.

Step 5. Discuss the results of the data you have now collected from your group. Do not defend your answers. Try to understand and be clear about what others and you are feeling. (All members are to try to help the group observe these guidelines.)

RECOMMENDED READING

A. Change in Communities

Alinsky, Saul. *Reveille for Radicals*. Chicago: University of Chicago Press, 1946.

Alinsky, Saul. *Rules for Radicals*. New York: Random House, 1971.

Bradford, Leland P. *Making Meetings Work*. La Jolla, California: University Associates, 1976.

Cox, Fred M. *Strategies of Community Organization*. Itasca, Illinois: F. E. Peacock, 1970.

Ecklein, J. L., and A. A. Lauffer. *Community Organizers and Social Planners*. New York: John Wiley & Sons, Inc., 1972.

Evry, Hal. *The Selling of a Candidate*. Los Angeles: Western Opinion Research Center, 1971.

Fessler, Donald R. *Facilitating Community Change*. La Jolla, California: University Associates, 1976.

Flanagan, Joan. *The Grass Roots Fund Raising Book*. Chicago: Swallow Press, 1977.

Grosser, C. F. *New Directions in Community Organization: From Enabling To Advocacy*. New York: Praeger, 1973.

Hallman, Howard W. *Government by Neighborhoods*. Washington, D.C.: Center for Governmental Studies, 1973.

Hallman, Howard. *The Organization and Operation of Neighborhood Councils*. New York: Praeger Publishers, Inc., 1977.

Hornstein, Benedict, Burke, Lewicki, and Hornstein. *Strategies for Social Change*. New York: Free Press, 1970.

Hornstein, et. al. *Social Intervention: A Behavioral Science Analysis*. New York: Free Press, 1971.

Jones, Mary H. *The Autobiography of Mother Jones*. New York: Charles H. Kerr, 1972.

Klein, Donald C. *Community Dynamics and Mental Health.* New York: John C. Wiley & Sons, Inc., 1968.

Kotler, Milton. *Neighborhood Government.* Indianapolis: Bobbs-Merrill Co., Inc., 1969.

Mayer, R. R. *Social Planning and Social Change.* Englewood Cliffs, New Jersey: Prentice-Hall, 1972.

Morris, David and Karl Hess. *Neighborhood Power: The New Localism.* Boston: Beacon Press, 1975.

Rothman, Jack. *Planning and Organization for Social Change: Action Principles from Social Science Research.* New York: Columbia Press, 1974.

Schaller, Lyle. *Community Organization: Conflict and Reconciliation.* Nashville: Abingdon Press, 1966.

Simpson, Dick. *Winning Elections.* Chicago: Swallow Press, 1976.

Simpson, Dick and George Beam. *Strategies for Change: How to Make the American Political Dream Work.* Chicago: Swallow Press, 1972.

Spiegel, Hans (ed.). *Citizen Participation in Urban Development.* Washington, D.C.: NTL Institute for Applied Behavioral Science, 1968.

Stevens Square Community Organization. *Stevens Square Design Plan.* Minneapolis: Stevens Square Community Organization, 1976.

Strauss, Bert and Mary E. Stowe. *How to Get Things Changed.* Garden City, New York: Doubleday & Company, Inc., 1974.

B.   CHANGE IN ORGANIZATIONS

Addison-Wesley Series on Organization Development (Reading, Mass.: 1969).

1) Beckhard. *Organization Development: Strategies and Models.*

2) Bennis, Warren. *Organization Development: Its Nature, Origins, and Prospects.*

3) Blake, R. R. and Jane Mouton. *Building A Dynamic Corporation Through Grid Organization Development.*

4) Lawrence and Lorsch. *Developing Organizations: Diagnosis and Action.*

5) Schein, Edgar H. *Process Consultation.*

6) Walton. *Interpersonal Peacemaking: Confrontations and Third Party Consultation.*

Argyris, Chris. *The Applicability of Organizational Sociology.* Cambridge, Mass.: University Press, 1972.

Argyris, Chris. *Integrating the Individual and the Organization.* New York: Wiley, 1964.

Argyris, Chris. *Intervention Theory and Method.* Reading, Mass.: Addison-Wesley, 1970.

Bennis, Warren. *Changing Organizations.* New York: McGraw-Hill, 1966.

Bennis, Warren, Kenneth Benne, and R. Chin. *The Planning of Change.* New York: Holt, Rinehart, and Winston, 1969.

Blake, R. R. and Jane Mouton. *Corporate Excellence Through Grid Organization Development.* Houston: Gulf Publishing Company, 1968.

Cummings, Thomas G. and Svivastva Survesh. *Management of Work: A Socio-Technical Systems Approach.* Kent, Ohio: Kent State University Press, 1977.

Drucker, Peter. *Management: Tasks, Responsibilities, Practices.* New York: Harper & Row, Publishers, 1974.

Eddy, Burke, Dupre, and South. *Behavioral Science and the Manager's Role.* Washington: NTL Institute, 1969.

Francis, Dave and Mike Woodcock. *People at Work: A Practical Guide to Organizational Change.* La Jolla: University Associates, 1975.

French, Wendell and Cecil H. Bell, Jr. *Organization Development.* Englewood Cliffs, New Jersey: Prentice-Hall, Inc., 1973.

Knudson, Harry R., Robert Woodworth, and Cecil H. Bell. *Management: Experiential Approach.* New York: McGraw Hill Book Company, 1973.

Kolb, David A., Ervin M. Rubin, and James M. McIntyre. *Organizational Psychology: An Experiential Approach*, 2nd edition. Englewood Cliffs, New Jersey: Prentice-Hall, 1974.

Lippit, Gordon. *Organizational Renewal.* New York: Appleton-Century-Crofts, 1969.

Lippit, Ron, J. Watson, and B. Westly. *The Dynamics of Planned Change.* New York: Harcourt, Brace, and World, 1958.

McConkey, Dale D. *MBO for Nonprofit Organizations.* New York: American Management Association, 1975.

Morrison, James H. *The Human Side of Management.* New York: Addison-Wesley Company, 1971.

Peter, Lawrence and Raymond Hull. *The Peter Principle.* New York: William Morrow & Company, Inc., 1969.

Schein, Edgar H. *Organizational Psychology.* Englewood Cliffs, New Jersey: Prentice-Hall, 1965.

Schein, Edgar and Warren Bennis. *Personal and Organizational Change Through Group Methods.* New York: John Wiley & Sons, 1965.

Schindler-Rainman, Eva and Ronald Lippitt. *Taking Your Meetings Out of the Doldrums.* Columbus, Ohio: Association of Professional Directors of the YMCA, 1975.

Sheane, Derrick. *Beyond Bureaucracy: The Future Shape and Transformation of Large, Complex Organizations.* London: Management Research, 1976.

Townsend, Robert. *Up the Organization.* Greenwich, Connecticut: Fawcett Crest Books, 1970.

C. HUMANISM AND HUMAN RELATIONS

Berne, Eric. *Games People Play.* New York: Grove Press, 1964.

Bradford, Leland. *Making Meetings Work.* La Jolla, California: University Associates, 1977.

Bradford, Leland, Jack Gibb, and Kenneth Benne. *T-Group Theory and Laboratory Method.* New York: John C. Wiley & Sons, 1965.

Dyer, Wayne W. *Your Erroneous Zones.* New York: Funk & Wagnalls, 1976.

Fast, Julius. *Body Language.* New York: Evans and Company, Inc., 1970.

Ford, Jr., D. L. *Readings in Minority Group Relations.* La Jolla, California: University Associates, 1975.

Golembiewski and Blumberg. *Sensitivity Training and the Laboratory Approach.* Itasca, Ill.: Peacock Publishers, Inc., 1970.

Gordon, Thomas. *Parent Effectiveness Training.* New York: P. H. Wyden, 1970.

Harris, Thomas A. *I'm OK, You're OK.* New York: Harper & Row, 1969.

James, William. *Humanism and Truth* (1917). From *The Works of William James.* Cambridge, Mass.: Harvard University Press, 1975.

Laing, R. D. *The Politics of Experience.* New York: Pantheon Books, 1967.

Laing, R. D. *Self and Others.* New York: Pantheon Books, 1970.

Maslow, Abraham. *Toward a Psychology of Being.* New York: Van Nostrand, 1962.

Miller, Sherod, Elam W. Nunnally, Daniel B. Wackman. *Alive and Aware: How to Improve Your Relationships Through Better Communication.* Minneapolis, Minnesota: Interpersonal Communication Programs, Inc., 1977.

Perls, Frederick. *In and Out the Garbage Pail.* Lafayette, Calif.: Real People Press, 1969.

Raths, Louis, Merrill Harmin, and Sidney Simon. *Values and Teaching.* Columbus, Ohio: Charles E. Merrill Company, 1966.

Rogers, Carl. *On Becoming a Person.* Boston: Houghton Mifflin Company, 1961.

Satir, Virginia. *Conjoint Family Therapy.* Palo Alto, Calif.: Science and Behavior Books, 1967.

Satir, Virginia. *Making Contact.* Millbrae, Calif.: Celestial Arts, 1976.

Satir, Virginia. *People Making.* Palo Alto, Calif.: Science and Behavior Books, 1972.

Schutz, William. *Here Comes Everybody.* New York: Harper & Row, 1971.

Wackman, Daniel B., Sherod Miller, Elam W. Nunnally. *Student Workbook: Increasing Awareness and Communication Skills.* Minneapolis, Minnesota: Interpersonal Communication Programs, Inc., 1977.

Watzlawick, Paul, et. al. *Change.* New York: W. W. Norton & Company, Inc., 1974.

D. ISSUES AND PERSPECTIVES

Abuse. Minneapolis: University of Minnesota, 1973.

Albert, Robert and Michael Emmons. *Your Perfect Right.* San Luis Obispo, Calif.: Impact, 1975.

Anderson, Robert, et. al. *Voices from Wounded Knee, 1973.* Akwesasne, New York: Akwesasne Notes, 1973.

Baldwin, James. *Another Country.* New York: Dial Press, 1962.

Bender, Tom. *Environmental Design Primer.* Denver: Environmental Action Reprint Service, 1973.

Bolles, Richard. *What Color Is Your Parachute: A Practical Manual for Job-Hunters and Career Changers.* New York: Ten Speed Press, 1977.

Commoner, Barry. *The Closing Circle.* New York: Alfred Knopf, 1971.

Conner, Desmond M. *Citizens Participate: An Action Guide for Public Issues.* Oakville, Ontario: Development Press, 1974.

Cox, Harvey. *The Secular City.* New York: Macmillan, 1966.

Deloria, Vine, Jr. *Behind the Trail of Broken Treaties.* New York: Dell Publishing Co., 1974.

De Rivera, Joseph. *Field Theory as Human Science.* New York: Gardner Press, Inc., 1976.

Druian, M. Greg. *Citizen Participation Handbook: Four Case Studies.* Portland: Northwest Regional Educational Laboratory, 1977.

Eiben, Ray and Al Milliren, editors. *Educational Change: A Humanistic Approach.* La Jolla: University Associates, 1976.

Firestone, Shulamith. *The Dialectic of Sex: The Case for Feminist Revolution.* New York: Morrow, 1970.

Fletcher, Joseph. *Situation Ethics.* Philadephia: Westminster Press, 1966.

Galbraith, John Kenneth. *The Affluent Society.* Boston: Houghton-Mifflin Company, 1976.

Galbraith, John Kenneth. *Economic Development.* Cambridge: Harvard University Press, 1964.

Gowan, Susanne. *Moving Toward a New Society.* Philadelphia: New Society Press, 1976.

Gregory, Dick. *Nigger.* New York: Dutton & Company, Inc., 1964.

Griffin, John. *Black Like Me.* New York: New American Library, 1961.

Hallman, Howard W. *Neighborhood Government in a Metropolitan Setting.* Beverly Hills: Sage Publications, 1974.

Hallman, Howard W. *The Organization and Operation of Neighborhood Councils.* New York: Praeger Publishers, 1977.

Handbook Collective, The. *The Food Co-op Handbook.* Denver: Environmental Action Reprint Service, 1975.

Harrington, Michael. *The Other America.* New York: Macmillan, 1962.

196   Appendix

Hodson, H. V. *The Dis-Economics of Growth.* Denver: Environmental Action
Reprint Service, 1973.

Hutchinson, Linda and Miriam Wasserman. *Teaching Human Dignity.* Minneapolis: Education Exploration Center, 1978.

Jacobs, Jane. *The Death and Life of Great American Cities.* New York: Random House, 1961.

King, Martin Luther, Jr. *Stride Toward Freedom.* New York: Harper & Row,
1958.

King, Martin Luther, Jr. *Where Do We Go From Here: Chaos or Community.*
New York: Harper & Row, 1967.

Knowles, Louis and Kenneth Prewitt. *Institutional Racism in America.*
Englewood Cliffs, New Jersey: Prentice-Hall, 1969.

Kotler, Milton. *Neighborhood Government: The Local Foundations of Political
Life.* Indianapolis: Bobbs-Merrill, 1960.

League of Women Voters. *Energy Dilemmas* and *Energy Options.* Washington,
D.C.: League of Women Voters Education Fund, 1977.

Lorrins, Amory. *World Energy Strategies: Facts, Issues, and Options.* Denver:
Environmental Action Reprint Service, 1975.

Malcolm X. *Autobiography.* New York: Grove Press, 1964.

Meadows, Donella, et. al. *The Limits to Growth,* 2nd ed. New York: Universe
Press, 1974.

Morgan, Robin. *Sisterhood Is Powerful: An Anthology of Writings from the
Women's Liberation Movement.* New York: Vintage, 1970.

Morris, David and Karl Hess. *Neighborhood Power: The New Localism.*
Boston: Beacon Press, 1975.

Moynihan, Daniel Patrick. *Maximum Feasible Misunderstanding.* New York:
Free Press, 1969.

Murray, Edward and Lee Webb, editors. *New Directions in State and Local
Public Policy.* Washington, D.C.: Conference on Alternative State and
Local Public Policies, 1977.

Nader, Ralph and Donald Ross. *Action for a Change.* New York: Grossman
Publishers, 1972.

Owens, Robert G. *Organizational Behavior in Schools.* Englewood Cliffs, New
Jersey: Prentice-Hall, Inc., 1970.

Sarason, S. B. *The Creation of Settings and the Future Societies.* New York:
Jossey-Bass, 1972.

Schumacher, E. F. *Small Is Beautiful.* New York: Harper Torchbooks, 1973.

Shalala, Donna E. *Neighborhood Governance: Issues and Proposals.* New
York: National Project on Ethnic America, 1971.

Simple Living Collective, The. *Taking Charge.* San Francisco: American
Friends Service Committee, 1977.

Simplified Parliamentary Procedures. Chicago: League of Women Voters,
1977.

Spiegel, Hans, B. C., editor. *Citizen Participation in Urban Development, Vols. I and II.* Washington, D.C.: Center for Community Affairs, 1968.

Stereotypes, Distortions, and Omissions in U. S. History Textbooks. (New York: Council on Interracial Books for Children, 1970.)

Terry, Robert. *For Whites Only.* Detroit: Detroit Industrial Mission, 1970.

Theobald, Robert. *Beyond Despair: Directions for America's Third Century.* Washington: New Republic Book Company, 1976.

Theobald, Robert. *Futures Conditional.* Indianapolis: Bobbs-Merrill, 1972.

Theobald, Robert. *Habit and Habitat.* New York: Prentice Hall, 1972.

Theobald, Robert. *Rich and Poor: A Study of the Economics of Rising Expectations.* New York: Potter, 1960.

Toffler, Alvin. *Future Shock.* New York: National General Company, 1971.

E. CONSCIOUSNESS

Bateson, Gregory. *Steps to an Ecology of Mind.* New York: Ballantine Books, Inc., 1975.

Boyd, Doug. *Rolling Thunder.* New York: Random House, 1974.

Boyd, Doug. *Swami.* New York: Random House, 1976.

Buber, Martin. *I and Thou.* New York: Charles Scribner's Sons, 1958.

Castaneda, Carlos. *Journey to Ixtlan.* New York: Simon & Schuster, 1972.

Castaneda, Carlos. *Tales of Power.* New York: Simon & Schuster, 1974.

Glasser, William. *Positive Addiction.* New York: Harper & Row, 1976.

Lame Deer, John and Richard Erdoes. *Lame Deer: Seeker of Visions.* New York: Simon & Schuster, 1972.

Maltz, Maxwell. *Psycho-Cybernetics.* Englewood Cliffs, N.J.: Prentice-Hall, 1960.

Moss, Thelma S. *The Probability of the Impossible.* Los Angeles, Tarcher, 1974.

Pearce, Joseph Chilton. *The Crack in the Cosmic Egg.* New York: Julian Press, 1971.

Pearce, Joseph Chilton. *Magical Child: Rediscovery of Nature's Plan for Our Children.* New York: E. P. Dutton & Co., 1975.

Pirsig, Robert. *Zen and the Art of Motorcycle Maintenance.* New York: William Morrow & Company, 1974.

Reich, Charles A. *The Greening of America.* New York: Random House, 1970.

Robbins, Tom. *Even Cowgirls Get the Blues.* Boston: Houghton-Mifflin, 1976.

Teilhard de Chardin, P. *The Phenomenon of Man.* New York: Harper & Row, 1959.

Thompson, Hunter S. *Fear and Loathing in Las Vegas.* New York: Random House, 1971.

INDEX